MARRIAGE
BY THE SPRIT
Rhythms of Grace

Fred and Sherry White

Published by Fountain Gate Publishers, Athens, GA USA
www.FountainGatePublishers.com

Printed in the Unites States of America

ISBN: 978-0-9826135-1-1

Dedication

This book is dedicated to all those who still hope for a better marriage, even though they may have been hurt in marriage. It is also dedicated to the thousands of men and women throughout the world whom we have taught and counselled about godly living. Foremost among these are our children and grandchildren and our spiritual sons and daughters. Their lives have blessed us greatly, and we want them to experience the fullness of life and marriage.

We gratefully acknowledge the work of the Holy Spirit in our lives, marriage and ministry. His grace strengthened us for life, enabling us to write. His enlightenment gave us something unique to say. This reference to the Spirit does not take away from our reliance on the Father and his Son, Jesus. Our relationship with the Spirit expanded and enriched our relationships with the Father and his Son. The guidance of the Spirit is evident throughout the book.

Fred and Sherry White

TABLE OF CONTENTS

PREFACE

Sherry and I (Fred) are high school sweethearts who are celebrating our fiftieth year of marriage (1964-2014). We often express our love to each other with the phrase "forever and a day" to show our undying love. We started dating when she was 15 and I was 17. Many of our dates consisted of going to church services together or working with cattle and horses. When I asked Sherry's father for permission to marry her, I assured him I owned cattle and would provide for her. He was not impressed, because he required Sherry to finish high school before getting married. She completed two years of high school credits in just one year to earn a high school diploma. We married after she graduated from high school and I completed a year of college. She was 17 and I was 19.

Beginning our married life together, we both attended a college 100 miles from our hometown. We had to depend on each other to start married life. It was a sharp departure from living in our hometown with family and old friends. After three years, we moved further away to continue our college education. We both earned undergraduate and graduate degrees and started working. We spent 12 years together before having children. Before having children, we had free time and extra money. We also played golf together and travelled to nearby cities for dinner and special occasions. Our relationship grew stronger as we spent time together and shared common interests.

We both had a call of God on our lives. To prepare for the call, we submitted to the Lord's authority, studied the word of God on our own and were taught by anointed ministers. Then we taught our revelation of Jesus Christ in many different venues in this country and elsewhere. We ventured out on our own by teaching children in low income areas. We had a mission for homeless people, prostitutes and addicts in our city for eight years. We financed the mission and other ministry activities on our own until others came alongside us to help. We ministered in different congregations, homes, jails, prisons and drug rehabilitation centers. Jesus healed, delivered and set the people free in these services. He changed the lives of people wherever he sent us.

When some of our family and friends were hurt in marriage, Sherry and I knew we needed to clear up some misunderstandings about marriage. We began writing on marriage from a spiritual perspective to help and encourage married couples. Some fundamental, but often misunderstood, truths about marriage were addressed in these early writings. We wrote about marriage to help young couples prepare for marriage and to teach married couples how to resolve marital problems and improve their marriage. The Spirit prompted us to write this book to explain our revelation about marriage and share our experiences to illustrate important principles. This book brings together our teachings and writings about marriage. This message is for anyone who is planning to marry or looking for a better married life. Though I will write my own voice, many of Sherry's insights will be included in the book.

In marriage we have experienced barrenness and fruitfulness, sicknesses and miracles, and death and life. We have seen the passing of generations and the birth of new ones. The book is not about our heartaches, but instead it attests to the wonderful rhythms of God's grace in marriage.

Purpose of the Book

The great mystery of marriage is revealed in this book. Understanding God's mysteries will help people stay free from deception and bondage. The book is intended for those who want to know the truth about marriage. If you read the book with an open heart, the Spirit will help you develop a vibrant and healthy marriage.

Spiritual marriages play a crucial role in the kingdom. This book explains the spiritual marriage by revelation of the Spirit and by practical experience. Praying together, studying the word of God together and working in the kingdom together will help you develop a spiritual marriage.

This book is filled with ideas and experiences to show readers the wonderful potential of marriage. Upon reading this book, you should be able to implement changes to improve your marriage. We hope you experience the wonders of marriage.

Organization of the Book

This book consists of four sections: the mystery of marriage, the foundation of marriage, the various types of marriage and the operation of a spiritual marriage. The first section introduces the mystery of marriage, which is characterized as a great mystery. It takes the Spirit to reveal the Father's mysteries. This section discusses the five distinguishing marks of a spiritual marriage: spirit, life, grace, purpose and destiny. These distinguishing marks are examined in the first three chapters.

The second section describes the foundation of a spiritual marriage. It is built on a sure foundation with a marriage covenant and three pillars of marriage. Chapter 4 introduces the marriage covenant based on the word of God and shows how God enriches the covenant by revelation of the Spirit. The next three chapters identify the three pillars upon which a spiritual marriage is built: love, intimacy and faith. Chapter 5 examines the spirit of love through courtship, engagement, marriage and maturity. Chapter 6 examines several areas of intimacy, including sexual, emotional, intellectual and spiritual. Chapter 7 examines faith which can grow from the size of a mustard seed to great faith. For those married couples facing problems related to love, intimacy and/or faith, Chapter 8 shows how to mend the pillars through forgiveness and blessings.

The third section compares three different types of marriage, prominently featuring a spiritual marriage as a radical departure from popular types. Several different types of marriage are possible with each having their own strengths and weaknesses. This section helps newlyweds choose the appropriate type of marriage and married couples identify the type of marriage in which they are living currently. Married couples may want to choose a different type of marriage on the basis of this discussion. Chapter 9 identifies the most popular types of marriage: worldly and carnal marriages. Chapter 10 examines the spiritual marriage.

The fourth section examines the operation of a spiritual marriage, emphasizing the role of the Spirit in marriage. Chapters 11-13 show how the husband and wife can become one in the flesh and one in the spirit. Specific instructions are offered for the husband and the wife. Chapter 14 discusses empowerment for a spiritual marriage. Chapter 15 discusses progress towards maturity in a spiritual marriage.

The final chapter of the book (chapter 16) reports some major conclusions. It shows how the concepts developed in this book can be applied in any marriage. The Spirit will show the husband and wife how to effectively apply the concepts.

Cover Image

The cover image symbolizes the book's title, Marriage by the Spirit: Rhythms of Grace. The two hearts depict a husband and wife joined together in marriage. The dove depicts the Spirit, indicating they walk in the spiritual realm. The heartbeat indicates the husband and wife are in harmony with each other and with the Spirit's rhythms of grace.

Preparation for Reading the Book

This book contains spiritual truths best understood when the reader's heart and mind are open and properly prepared. Be willing to lay down any preconceived ideas on marriage not pleasing to the Lord. Prayer helps prepare the heart and mind to receive revelation from the Spirit. The better prepared in prayer you are, the more revelation you will gain. Ask the Lord for a fresh revelation on marriage. Expect a fire in your passion for the Lord and your spouse to be ignited.

Chapter 1
MYSTERY OF MARRIAGE:
SPIRIT AND LIFE

Entering marriage may seem mysterious and formidable, but the Spirit has been sent to show the way. Many couples spend several months planning their wedding without adequately preparing for their marriage. The mystery is not the wedding but the marriage. The marriage relationship is a great mystery, illustrating the spiritual marriage of Christ and his church (Ephesians 5:32). This chapter introduces the concept of a spiritual marriage and identifies five distinguishing marks of a spiritual marriage. These distinguishing marks are life, spirit, grace, purpose and destiny. Life and spirit are addressed in this chapter; grace is addressed in chapter 2; and purpose and destiny are addressed in chapter 3.

Introducing the Spiritual Marriage

Man's thoughts are natural or soulish so he only understands a natural form of marriage, but God is spirit and he has ordained marriage of a spiritual nature. It takes revelation of the word of God by the Spirit to distinguish between a natural marriage and a spiritual marriage.

A natural marriage is based on natural emotions and feelings of love and physical attractions. Natural people and even carnal Christians can have a natural marriage without ever acknowledging the existence of a supernatural God or calling on him for help. For example, many people talk about marrying their soul mate, but the concept of a soul mate is in the natural or soulish realm rather than the spiritual realm. "But a natural man does not accept the things of the Spirit of God, for they are foolishness to him; and he cannot understand them, because they are spiritually appraised" (1 Corinthians 2:14). In some cases a man and woman may enter marriage outside of the will of God, and thus he does not join them together.

God joins a man and woman together in spiritual marriage by breathing life into the marriage. The spirit of the husband and the spirit of the wife are divinely united to fulfill the purpose of the Lord. Spiritual marriage is ordained of the Lord. Man must never separate a husband and wife whom God has joined together (Mark 10:9). In spiritual marriage, both the husband and wife are led by the Spirit. A spiritual marriage is the divine union of two spirit beings who are being led by the Spirit.

Spiritual marriages grow and change over time. These five distinguishing marks help explain how spiritual marriages are different from natural marriages.

- Spiritual marriages are spirit and life, implying they can be changed. Such changes occur throughout the life of the marriage.
- Spiritual marriages are grace relationships. Grace calls for continual changes in lives and marriages. Also, grace

empowers a husband and wife to change their lives and their marriage.

- Spiritual marriages make changes to discover purpose and fulfill destiny. The purpose for each marriage has been in the heart of God from the beginning. Destiny for marriage is the lifelong path married couples follow to fulfill God's purpose for their marriage.

Spirit and Life

Marriage is a building block of the Church, and it is an expression of the family of God. Marriage was never intended to be an inanimate object or a lifeless institution. The thought of an institution implies confinement and restrictions. Marriage is intended to be an expression of God's love operating in the eternal relationship of Christ and his bride. The ultimate spiritual marriage is Christ in his fullness living through his bride, the church. Hence, each spiritual marriage involves the expression of Christ in both the husband and wife by his living in them and through them.

Spiritual marriage is spirit and life. The heavenly Father is spirit, and he is the Father of spirits (John 4:24 and Hebrews 12:9). His children are described as spirits with souls and bodies. Those who reverence the Father must do it out of their very being, their spirits, their true selves (John 4:24 MSG). The word of God is spirit and life (John 6:63). His word ordains marriage, making it spirit and life. If marriage has life then it can grow and change. Its changes are not linear in nature but rhythmic like music.

As spirit, the spiritual marriage is more like the Lord than either man or woman. It expresses both masculine and feminine attributes just as the Lord himself. He is both the man of war and the nursing mother. His name Jehovah Sabaoth, which is translated as the Lord of Armies, denotes he is sovereign ruler over every army. His name El Shaddai refers to the Lord who freely gives nourishment and supplies the needs of his people as a mother would her child. A spiritual marriage is powerful and yet gracious providing protection to those under its authority and sustenance to many.

Life comes from the breath of God, which is his Spirit. God breathes on a person by his Spirit and the spirit within the person comes alive. The new life of the Spirit is spiritual. Flesh can birth only flesh, but the Spirit gives birth to spirit (John 3:6). God breathes on a marriage and life comes into the marriage. A spiritual marriage is different from other marriages. It is vibrant and strong. It survives the greatest trials.

Each believer is made up of three parts - spirit, soul and body. The spirit is the innermost being of a believer. The scriptures often refer to the innermost being as spirit of man regardless of whether the believer is male or female. This term spirit is not capitalized to distinguish the innermost being from the Spirit of God which is capitalized. Since this book is intended for both men and women, we prefer using an alternative to the term spirit of man. We use the terms spirit, spirit of the believer or spirit of beauty to refer to the innermost being of either a man or a woman. Peter wrote, "Your beauty ... should be that of your inner self, the unfading beauty of a gentle and quiet spirit" (1 Peter 3:3-4 NIV).

There are a few important things known about the spirit of a believer. The spirit of a believer is recreated by the Spirit and adopted into the family of God. What does this mean? First, the spirit of a believer cries out for the things of God. You have received a spirit of adoption by which you cry out, "Abba, Father!" (Romans 8:15b).The spirit will seek those things above where Christ is seated (Colossians 3:1-2). The spirit yearns for fellowship with the Lord.

Second, the general purpose of the spirit of a believer is to yield fruit for the Lord. This fruit includes love, joy, peace, patience, kindness, goodness, faithfulness, gentleness and self-control (Galatians 5:22-23). When believers catch hold of what their spirit says then their mind becomes renewed and fruitful.

Third, the spirit of a believer must be liberated to fulfill purpose and destiny. It takes the Spirit to free and energize the spirit of a believer. The Spirit brings freedom (2 Corinthians 3:17). The more believers communicate with the Spirit the freer their spirit becomes. People who experience the new birth still have to be loosed from all the things keeping them in bondage.

As believers understand the word of God, they are able to distinguish their spirit from their soul. It takes the word of God to divide the spirit from the soul and the spiritual from the natural (Hebrews 4:12). Seek God's kingdom first and all your needs will be met (Matthew 6:33). Also, prayer is critical for releasing the spirit of a believer. Believers can operate a vibrant prayer life by studying the prayers shown in the word of God. However, just repeating these prayers does not ensure the spirit of a believer will be brought forth in fullness. Reliance on the Spirit is needed for the full development of the spirit of a believer.

Personal Story – Overcoming Adversities

Sherry and I married soon after graduating from high school. We were both young; she was 17 and I was 19. Our marriage started as a fragile natural relationship, but it changed over the last 50 years to a vibrant spiritual marriage.

It would be very hard for anyone to live with me. I am goal oriented and disciplined, demanding much from myself and from others. This example from my childhood may help explain my personality. My little sister and I raised steers together. I was disciplined in my care for the steers, and I required her to do the same things I did. My sweet little sister got so mad at me for requiring so much from her, she hit me over the head with a croquet mallet. Even though she may not recall the incident, I still have a knot on my head to prove it. The Lord has renewed my mind and made my spirit more sensitive to spiritual things, but I still have the same personality. I know it has been a miracle for Sherry to love me and stay married to me for 50 years.

Together Sherry and I have faced many difficulties in marriage. Whenever we faced trouble, we always sought the Lord more diligently than before. We have dealt with barrenness, cancer and heart problems just to name a few. The doctors said it was not possible for us to have children. Then when the Lord miraculously gave us a daughter, the doctors said she was going to die, but the Lord intervened again. In 1992, the doctors said Sherry had cancer and would live no more than six months, but they did not know the Lord would deliver her from cancer. Sherry, who has been sensitive to the spiritual realm from an early age, has been frequently and openly attacked by demonic forces. Three times demonic forces drove her to the brink of suicide. The Lord always miraculously intervened on our behalf to save her life. During her last suicide attempt, the children and I were huddled together in prayer for her. Our daughter told the Lord her mother hears his voice and asked him to send her home from wherever she was. The Lord told Sherry her life was not her own but she had been purchased by his blood. Then he told her to pour out both the pills and the water and return to her family. Marriage may not be easy, but regardless of the costs of sustaining the marriage it is worth it all.

Looking back over the last 50 years, we can identify when and how our marriage changed. We attribute these changes to no man. In fact, nothing we were taught about marriage by man turned out to be meaningful. Instead, the Spirit taught us and led us in developing a spiritual marriage. He freed our spirits to grow, follow him and fulfill destiny. Now, we travel over the world to teach, preach and demonstrate the kingdom of God.

Concluding Remarks

A spiritual marriage is a unique expression of the Lord himself for he has breathed himself into the marital relationship between a man and woman. He has turned a natural relationship into spirit and life. A spiritual marriage is more powerful and more glorious than just the man and woman who make up the marriage. It is an expression of the Lord's increase for he adds himself to the relationship. The husband and wife are one with each other and one with the Lord.

Chapter 2
GRACE JOINTS

Spiritual relationships are built with grace. "But grow in the grace and knowledge of our Lord and Savior Jesus Christ" (2 Peter 3:18a). The power of God is embodied in his Spirit, who is also known as the Spirit of grace (Zechariah 12:10 and Hebrews 10:29). Grace can be defined as the active power or energy of the Spirit operating through a believer. Any relationship built on grace can be called a grace relationship, and a marriage built on grace is one of the strongest expressions of grace relationships. A marriage built on grace can withstand the storms of life. This chapter shows how to build and sustain spiritual marriages with God's grace.

Spiritual relationships are built only on the Lord's ordained joints. These relationships are built with grace and called grace joints. The phrase "whom God joins together" is frequently used in weddings, even though it is not well understood. Many couples marry without being joined together by the Lord. He does not join a believer to an unbelievers (2 Corinthians 6:14). In some cases, two believers can marry and still not be joined by the Lord.

Introduction to Grace Joints

The Spirit revealed the concept of grace joints to help Sherry and me understand how to build spiritual relationships. As we ministered to several Christians, the Spirit revealed they were not joined to us in ministry. Several years ago, a 12-year-old girl named Adrian prayed for the Lord to send someone to teach her about Jesus. The Spirit moved on Sherry and me to go to Adrian's community and teach the children about Jesus. We led Adrian and her family and friends to the Lord. Later Adrian became a missionary to Mexico. Also, we taught the word of God to adults in Adrian's community. More people came to our services than could be seated in the little building we were using. We rented a larger building for outreach a few blocks away, thinking many of these Christians would go with us. However, the Spirit said we were not joined with any of those people in Adrian's community but we could only build on joints in the body of Christ. I argued with the Spirit, because we had led those people to the Lord and taught them the word of God. But he was right, and I was wrong. None of those people went with us to the larger building even though it was within walking distance from the first, small building. Our ministry grew but not with those people, because the Lord had not joined them with us. He had other joints for them, and they had to follow the Spirit to find their own joints. It takes the Spirit to reveal the ordained joints where spiritual building occurs. Every marriage is not an ordained joint, but those marriages ordained of the Lord are destined to be spiritual marriages.

Understanding Grace

Grace relationships are built on the joints, which are those believers whom God supernaturally connects. The body of Christ is knit together by what every joint supplies (Ephesians 4:16 and Colossians 2:19). When each individual part does its share, God increases the body. Likewise, God increases a marriage when both the husband and wife do their share. To help understand the operation of grace several opposing concepts will be addressed. This approach will help clarify what grace is and what it is not.

Enable versus Empower

Grace empowers people to change. Just as it took grace to make Paul an apostle and a spiritual father, it takes grace to make a spiritual marriage. Grace produced the spiritual Paul and empowered him to do all he did (1 Corinthians 15:10). Pouring God's grace into a relationship empowers people to advance towards him. Grace does not just enable them to continue doing the same things they have always done. Without grace, pouring more money and other resources into a relationship just enables people to continue along the same path they have been travelling. Only by grace can a marriage flourish and move forward.

Container versus Channel

Grace flows better through an open channel benefiting others than a closed container benefiting only one person. In marriages built on grace both the husband and wife become channels of grace, contributing grace to the marriage through their words and actions. The relationship is not simply a grace container functioning like a gas tank for one of the marriage partners to be refilled continuously in order to keep the relationship alive. If only one spouse serves as a channel of grace, he/she will become fatigued. In a spiritual marriage both the husband and wife are generous with the grace God has given them. It is gracious for a husband to treat his wife as someone special rather than property he owns and controls. Marriage does not give a husband the right to mistreat or abuse his wife or lord his authority over her. Likewise, it is gracious for a wife to treat her husband as someone special rather than resenting his authority or appearing to be unhappy with his presence and help. Husbands and wives operating in grace are led by the Spirit of grace and strengthened by grace. Such grace relationships are supernatural in nature and stronger than natural relationships. Even when difficulties arise in a grace relationship, neither the husband nor the wife will abandon the relationship but allow the Spirit of grace to reconcile them.

Pride versus Humility

Grace operates through humility, but it is blocked by pride. Humility prepares believers to receive grace from the Lord. He gives grace to the humble (James 4:6). Humility involves giving up your identity to take on Christ's identity. He laid down his life to purchase sinners out of the world. He washed them by his blood and perfected them by his love to be his bride. Their iniquities and unfaithfulness did not diminish his love for his bride. He loves his bride with an unfailing love. He is motivated by compassion for his bride.

If believers humble themselves, Christ will be exalted in them. Christ is manifested in the lives of believers through the work of the Spirit. Humility is an attitude about God rather than an attitude about oneself. Humility recognizes a person's dependence on God. It takes God's perspectives and adopts God's ways. Believers are changed into the image of God's Son as they look at Jesus, not by looking at their faults, even when they are trying to correct them.

Humility begins at home. How can a person walk in humility before the invisible God without walking in humility before his/her spouse? Humility in marriage is similar to humility before God. It involves exalting your spouse, not abasing yourself. It values your spouse's feelings and opinions.

Humility reaches out for help from the body of Christ, but pride needs no help from anyone. Isolation from the body of Christ is prideful and harmful to the marriage. Couples should never get to the point where they have no need to be joined to the body of Christ (1 Corinthians 12:21-22). A married couple needs to be actively involved in the body of Christ, seeking spiritual support and guidance from anointed believers.

Humility in a marriage means that both the husband and wife are teachable. They are not rigid in their thinking but willing to learn and adjust. They are humble when they seek the Lord's guidance, being quick to hear and respond to his guidance. They are willing to be transparent with no hidden agendas and no manipulation. A husband is humble when he listens to his wife. A wife is humble when she lets the husband lead. Humility prays and recognizes the need for the Spirit's guidance. Like humility before God, humility in marriage yields benefits, such as grace, which strengthens the marriage.

Grace Attributes

Five important attributes of grace are described below.

Grace Reconciles Relationships

The reconciling force of grace is a fundamental force in building a strong relationship. Through the free gift of grace by Jesus Christ many are reconciled to God and made right with him (Romans 5:10 and 15). Believers can stand confidently in a relationship of grace, knowing God is their Father and he has glorious things for them. The supernatural realm becomes open and accessible to them. Believers have access to the heavenly throne of grace where they can obtain grace, as well as mercy and help (Hebrews 4:16). Thus believers can obtain more grace by spending more time at the throne of grace in the presence of the Lord. As believers experience more of the supernatural realm, they will walk in greater power. Operating in God's grace is evidence a person has experienced the supernatural realm.

Grace Invites the Presence of the Spirit

Words of encouragement will invite the Spirit into a situation, but hurtful or foul language will drive him away (Ephesians 4:29-30). It is possible to welcome and receive the Spirit of grace and then see him change situations. On the other hand, it is possible to grieve the Spirit of grace and see him depart from a situation. When the Spirit has removed himself from a situation, believers can either continue to operate in the same situation with only natural abilities or follow the Spirit and leave. Continuing to operate only with natural abilities will make any problem worse, but following the Spirit will lead to peace and victory. The Spirit of grace abides where there is peace, love, harmony and faith. Relationships flourish in this positive environment.

Grace Strengthens in Times of Weakness

Believers will find their natural abilities are inadequate to build strong relationships. Even when believers are weak, God's grace is powerful. His grace is perfected in weakness (2 Corinthians 12:9). As long as believers function where they have grace, they will be able to build strong relationships, stand against attacks of the enemy and walk in victory. When marriages are under pressure or temptations abound, a husband and wife need strength to endure. Grace strengthens them to move forward without yielding to temptations.

Grace Serves Others

Use grace to serve others (1 Peter 4:10). Marriage partners can serve their spouse through gracious words and gracious actions by speaking and acting on the word of God. The words of a wise man are gracious and win him favor (Ecclesiastes 10:12 AMP). A husband and wife operating in grace know how to answer for the hope within them. They do not need to plan what to say. The Spirit will fill their mouth with the words of the Father (Matthew 10:18-20). Knowing what the Father would have a husband or wife say in a particular situation is an operation of grace. The word of God is full of grace and truth (John 1:14), and it is even called the word of grace (Acts 14:3 and 20:32). God's grace supernaturally empowers and energizes a husband and wife to serve one another. Marriage partners cannot effectively minister grace to their spouse until they have received grace and operated in it.

The eyes of faith see the future, but it takes grace to build it. For all future time God will show the riches of his grace by being kind to us in Christ Jesus (Ephesians 2:7). When people look at any situation through natural eyes, they may see obstacles and impossibilities; but when they are strengthened with grace, they can see the possibilities and achieve great things. Look beyond present circumstances and begin to fashion the future for yourself and your spouse by relying on grace to supernaturally overcome natural situations and change circumstances.

Rhythms of Grace

Different seasons and rhythms in marriage bring changes. For example, a married couple faces different issues before having children than they do while parenting infants and teenagers. Many people do not respond well to such changes, but the Spirit can help people deal with them. Those who have the Spirit can receive strength and guidance from the Spirit, but those without the Spirit cannot understand the things of the Spirit. If the seasons and rhythms are not understood and properly dealt with the marriage may be adversely affected. Marriages can thrive year after year by following the Spirit and riding on waves of grace. The great mystery of marriage involves the dynamic rhythm of grace. Jesus invited all those who are weary to come to him for rest and to "learn the unforced rhythms of grace" (Matthew 11:28-30 MSG). Discover the rhythms of spiritual marriage.

Rhythms are like the waves, tides and currents of the sea. Winds, differences in temperature and movement of the moon control the rhythms of the sea. The tide is a great wave of water following the moon. While the rhythms of the sea are controlled by these natural elements, the supernatural rhythms are controlled by the Spirit. He is the one who controls the rhythms of life. There are seasons to build and seasons to refrain from building. "There is an appointed time for everything" (Ecclesiastes 3:1). It is possible to know the times and what ought to be done (1 Chronicles 12:32). Spiritual people know because they are led by the Spirit.

Philip followed the Spirit and flowed with the rhythms of grace. He ministered to the crowds in Samaria with great power. "The crowds with one accord were giving attention to what was said by Philip, as they heard and saw the signs which he was performing" (Acts 8:6). He could have stayed in the city and ministered to the crowds, but he would have missed the wave of grace being poured out on the Ethiopian as he travelled on the desert road. Philip left the city to minister to one person, because he was led by the Spirit. He led the Ethiopian into salvation and baptized him in water. "When they came up out of the water, the Spirit of the Lord snatched Philip away" (Acts 8:39a). Nothing compares to being sensitive to the Spirit and flowing in his rhythms of grace.

God gives each believer a new heart and strengthens the heart with grace. His grace, mixed with faith and love in Christ Jesus, overflows in abundance (1 Timothy 1:14). Grace is the heartbeat of God. It moves in rhythms like waves, bringing salvation to those who believe. Some believers may know when they are in the wave of grace and when they are not in it, but staying in the wave is a different matter. Sensitivity to the Spirit is needed to stay in the wave. It is especially important for married couples to follow the

Spirit and stay immersed in the wave of grace. Only by grace will the marriage be strengthened to move forward in the spiritual realm.

Marriage can have both natural and spiritual rhythms. Rhythms are developed around schedules for working, eating, sleeping, recreating, etc. These rhythms can change over time and through the seasons of life. Newlyweds may work at identifying and establishing rhythms in marriage, but such rhythms are often fragile and easily broken. Christ gave the five-fold ministry gifts to train believers in serving one another until they are mature adults moving rhythmically with each other in response to God's Son (Ephesians 4:7-13 MSG). As mutual trust is developed in marriage, the rhythms of marriage may go to a higher level. When the rhythms of life for a husband and wife come together, it is like a beautiful symphony.

Personal Story - Marriage Rhythms

Sherry and I adopted unique rhythms of the marriage in order for both of us to go to graduate school at different times. She graduated from college and took a job while I was working on my dissertation in graduate school. During the day, I wrote on the dissertation and she worked in an office. In the evening, we worked together; she typed various drafts of my dissertation and I made revisions. Each evening after finishing work, we would go out for a snack. We kept a consistent but demanding schedule. While I was working at the university, Sherry began her graduate education. In the daytime, I worked at the university and she cared for our children; in the evening she took university classes and I cared for our children. Each evening after she returned home from her classes, I would go back to the university to work for a few more hours. Our neighbors thought I was working at a second job in the evenings, because we kept such a consistent schedule. We adjusted our schedules for months at a time to help each other.

Spiritual rhythms were also established in our marriage. When doctors said our daughter was going to die, we turned our world upside down to pursue God and his solution to her health problems. It meant putting God first in our lives. We left the congregation we were attending and started travelling to a congregation in another town to learn more about God's healing. We spent much time in studying the word of God and attending conventions where God's healing was taught. We focused on God's healing and followed a healing wave wherever the Spirit carried us. He heard the cries of our heart and healed our daughter. There was a rhythm of grace for healing established in our lives. The wave of healing grace continues to be strong in our thinking, our lives and our ministry. No longer are we just seeking healing waves, but we carry them to the nations with signs and wonders following us.

Concluding Remarks

For the husband and wife who are concerned they went ahead of God and married without him joining them together, it is not too late. Jesus Christ can repair the breach and redeem your marriage. Trust in him to redeem your situation, and you will be carried into dimensions in the spiritual realm never before imagined.

Both the husband and wife have to operate in grace for the marriage to be considered a grace marriage. Operating in grace means a person is led by the Spirit of grace and strengthened by grace. Grace marriages are supernatural relationships which make them stronger than natural relationships. No matter what difficulties the married couple face, God's grace is sufficient for overcoming the difficulties. When difficulties arise in a grace marriage, neither the husband nor the wife will abandon the relationship. Instead, the married couple will allow the Spirit of grace to reconcile them. Grace marriages are highly valued in the kingdom of God, having eternal significance.

Chapter 3
PURPOSE AND DESTINY

In a spiritual marriage, both the husband and wife are led by the Spirit to discover God's purpose for them and their marriage. As they do God's will and accomplish his purpose, they touch eternity and bring heaven to bear on earth and fulfill destiny.

Discovering Purpose

Purpose has been in the heart of God from the beginning. He has a specific purpose for every person and every ordained marriage. His purposes are hidden but can be discovered by those who seek to know them through the Spirit. God's purposes for a husband and wife and their marriage are all linked together. His purpose for the marriage cannot be discovered apart from discovering his purposes for both the husband and the wife.

God's purpose is programmed inside each person like genetic instructions. A person's unique purpose in God has to be discovered. Rely on God's Spirit to decode his purposes for you, your spouse and your marriage. The purposes of God can only be understood with the Spirit's help (1 Corinthians 2:14). "Ask, and it will be given to you; seek, and you will find; knock, and it will be opened to you" (Matthew 7:7). Keep asking, seeking and knocking to discover your unique God-ordained purpose. Discovering God's purpose is a life-long pursuit.

Adopting someone else's view of purposes is not the same as letting the Spirit reveal them to you. Let no one try to make you conform to his/her own purpose. Some ministers try to develop many followers who are all alike. They want their followers to catch their vision for life. God's ministers should help believers discover his ordained purposes for them and their marriage.

The lives of believers are not a book filled with blank pages on which others can write in order to specify purpose. The book about believers has already been written. "Behold, I have come (in the scroll of the book it is written of me) to do your will, O God" (Hebrews 10:7). Believers can find what is written in the word of God about them and their marriage as the scriptures are made alive by the Spirit. The Spirit will paint a unique picture of purpose for each believer and each marriage. Scriptures are brought to life through revelation to show the picture of God's purpose.

Fulfilling Destiny

While purpose relates to God's plan for a person, destiny relates to a person's response to God's purpose. Destiny involves embracing and accomplishing God's purpose. Destiny does the will of the Father, accomplishing his purpose. Some general elements about the destiny of all believers are given in the word of God, but the specific elements of destiny for an individual are revealed by the Spirit. For example, all believers are destined to be conformed to the family image of Jesus Christ (Romans 8:29). Jesus only spoke the words he heard the Father say and only did those things he saw the Father do (John 5:19 and 8:26-28). The destiny for all believers involve speaking the words they hear the Father say and doing those things they see the Father do.

God's destiny for each married couple involves accomplishing his purpose. God joins a man and woman in marriage to fulfill destiny. Marriage opens up additional dimensions of destiny for a married couple unavailable to either the man or woman in isolation. For example, God made a covenant with Abraham (then Abram) making him the first patriarch of God's chosen people (Genesis 15:1-4). Initially, God did not specify who the first matriarch would be. Since his wife Sarah (then Sarai) was childless, Abraham thought the covenant could be fulfilled by his having a son with another woman (Genesis 16:15 and 17:18). God revealed the covenant would be fulfilled with a son from his own wife, Sarah (Genesis 17:15-16). Thus Sarah became the first matriarch of God's chosen people, indicating God's promise to the husband extended to the wife, as well. If two in agreement ask for something in prayer, the Father will do it (Matthew 18:19). No one would qualify for this powerful promise in isolation.

The spirit of a believer understands things the intellectual mind does not understand. In particular, the spirit can have an understanding of a believer's purpose and destiny the carnal mind cannot comprehend. For who among men knows the thoughts of a man except the spirit of the man which is in him? (1 Corinthians 2:11a) Both the growth and liberation of the spirit are important for destiny to be fulfilled. The spirit receives nourishment for growth from the milk of the word of God and the meat of the word (1 Peter 2:2 and Hebrews 5:12-14).

Personal Story - One Spirit and One Destiny

Sherry's purpose was revealed by the Spirit. At the age of nine she knew she was being sent to preach the gospel all over the world. Although I accepted Jesus as my savior at the age of 13, I discovered my true purpose as an adult through several encounters with Jesus. I was instructed to teach his people how to follow the Spirit and fulfill their destiny. Our purpose has been clarified over the years as we developed personal relationships with the Spirit, studied the word of God, pursued relationships with spiritual people and sought to know the Father's will for our lives.

The Lord's purpose for Sherry and me as a married couple is to spread the gospel of the kingdom. He has given us the authority and responsibility to teach and write about marriage, as well as several other areas including faith and relationship building. Our gifts and callings to write are grounded in Jesus' teachings. He sends prophets, apostles, wise men and scribes (Matthew 23:34 and Luke 11:29). The reason for his sending these gifts to the body of Christ is to teach the truth to believers and free them from the traditions of men, which allows them to operate in their true authority. Scribes are writing gifts who operate with the other gifts of prophets, apostles and wise men. All of these gifts are evident in our lives and ministries, allowing us to write with authority. Our writings inspire and encourage believers in the things of God.

Sherry and I began teaching about marriage in small groups and in marriage seminars. Then we wrote about marriage in more detail to follow up on these sessions and to prepare in-depth materials for counseling on marriage. We distributed these materials through videos posted on the Internet, booklets and blog posts. We drew from these earlier materials in writing this book, but there is much more detail and depth about marriage presented herein than in any of the materials we have elsewhere. Our writings on marriage are a part of our destiny and legacy.

Concluding Remarks

Purpose for every person is found in the heart of God. The only way to discover things in God's heart is through his Spirit. The Father's Spirit knows what is in his own heart and will reveal purpose to all those who seek to know it. Doing anything other than God's purpose would be a good work at best, but good works do not touch eternity. People are easily frustrated and fatigued in doing good works. Joy and satisfaction come from finding God's purpose and fulfilling destiny. A married couple operating only in good works will not have the strength to endure unto the end. By seeking to know God's purpose for the marriage and pursuing destiny, both the husband and wife are strengthened by the Spirit for this life, as well as the age to come.

Chapter 4
MARRIAGE COVENANT

Understanding the marriage covenant can help people bravely enter marriage without the fear of losing freedom. With a marriage covenant, a man and woman can walk in more freedom together after the wedding than before. Both pre-marital and marital relationships are contrasted to explain how a married couple can walk in freedom. The marriage covenant considered in this chapter centers around Christ. It has three important pillars: love, intimacy and faith. The love of Christ is addressed in chapter 5; intimacy is addressed in chapter 6; and faith is addressed in chapter 7. Forgiveness can be used to help mend any of these pillars; it is addressed in chapter 8. The marriage covenant as discussed in these five chapters can help a married couple adjust to the challenges of change and deal with marital problems.

Typically in courtship, the man lavishes attention on the woman, and the woman is sensitive to the man. However, there are no widely accepted norms of behavior during courtship. If the behavior of either the man or woman is unacceptable relative to the other person's desired norms, the relationship may be jeopardized. These desired norms of behavior are seldom explained or understood, making the status of the relationship uncertain for both parties. Not knowing what behavior is acceptable to the other person can create problems. Carrying these same concerns into the marriage could cause further problems. Some of these uncertainties can be resolved by the man and woman agreeing on their wedding vows related to desired behavior. These vows could become the standard or marriage covenant by which the man and woman live together.

Introduction

The marriage covenant is a supernatural promise or agreement between a husband and wife. It brings freedom, fulfillment and abundance. God's unconditional love is the foundation of his marriage covenant. Unconditional love is the richest and most satisfying form of love, but bringing romance into a marriage is good. God speaks specifically about the marriage covenant in the 5th chapter of Ephesians, verses 21 through 33. It begins with submitting one to another (Ephesians 5:21). Once two people enter into a covenant, no man can add to it or take from it. Let no man break apart what God has joined together (Matthew 19:6). The Spirit can continue to reveal the marriage covenant to the married couple through time. When my wife and I first married, we had very little understanding of the marriage covenant. As we developed a deeper understanding of the word of God and a better relationship with the Spirit, we understood the marriage covenant better and could activate the covenant in our own marriage.

The marriage covenant is not written in stone but engraved on the hearts of the husband and wife. Just like other Christian covenants, it is "written not with ink but with the Spirit of the living God, not on tablets of stone but on tablets of human hearts"

(2 Corinthians 3:3b). The marriage covenant embodies God's truth about marriage. The truth sets believers free (John 8:32). Using the word of God to control and manipulate a spouse is a perversion of the marriage covenant. The guidance of the Spirit brings freedom to the marriage. "Where the Spirit of the Lord is, there is liberty" (2 Corinthians 3:17b).

A few components of our marriage covenant will be identified to help others understand the marriage covenant. Some of the foundation components for our marriage covenant include the husband cherishing the wife and the wife honoring and reverencing the husband. Both of these concepts are found in the fifth chapter of Ephesians. My wife is an equal partner in this covenant. She helps me with decisions related to marriage, family and ministry and then offers her abilities freely.

Framework for Coping with Change

A marriage covenant provides a framework for a husband and wife to cope with changes in their relationship. The changes every married couple experiences over time could cause problems in the relationship. These changes could relate to finances, employment and careers; children; physical and emotional problems; extended family, etc. When a marriage is based solely on romantic love, the marriage partners are often unable to deal successfully with major changes. The pressures of change could cause a marriage based solely on carnal things to end in divorce.

A marriage covenant based on the word of God provides a powerful framework to cope with change. Sherry and I had no children for the first twelve years of marriage, but afterwards we

MARRIAGE BY THE SPIRIT

had three children in a span of three years. Children meant a big change for us. We raised our children in the training and admonition of the Lord (Ephesians 6:4). We were partners in raising the children. Sherry took care of the children while I worked, and I took care of the children while she completed a master's degree and started her own business. If it had not been for the Lord, our marriage might have been destroyed as we faced numerous challenges with a growing family.

The marriage covenant is broad enough to make provision for divorce in extreme cases. Adultery can be used as grounds for divorce (Matthew 5:32). Also, abandonment can be used as grounds for divorce. If an unbeliever insists on leaving the relationship, let him/her leave (1 Corinthians 7:15). Some partners try to justify divorce by claiming there is no longer any love in the relationship. However, the marriage covenant makes no provision for a man to divorce his wife simply because he no longer loves her or she no longer loves him. Even when the married couple's love for each other seems to fail, the marriage covenant is strong enough to rebuild the marriage and cause it to flourish under the guidance of the Spirit.

Personal Story ‑ My Three Wives

I often joke about having lived with three wives. First, I fell in love with Sherry who was seventeen and full of life. When we wed in 1964, we both had high school diplomas but no job skills. We were naïve about the things of this world and the things of God. This was the woman with whom I expected to spend my life. Then Sherry studied at three universities and received undergraduate and graduate degrees in business education. She taught at a vocational college. After 12 years of marriage, we adopted our first son. She resigned from the teaching position in order to spend more time at home with our son. In a short period of time, we had two other children. Then Sherry developed a career to accommodate being a wife and the mother of three children. She developed her own training business and her own jewelry business. She traveled through several states training business managers and government officials. Thus, my second wife, Sherry, was an educated professional and a successful entrepreneur. I loved her too, but she was far different from the one I wed. In more recent years Sherry has become an emissary of the kingdom and a powerful prophetess of God. She is a spiritual person who has great influence in the body of Christ. We travel over the world together ministering the gospel of the kingdom. My third wife, Sherry, is a seasoned minister of God carrying revival fires to the nations. She is far different from the woman I wed, but I greatly love her. If I could only love my wife as she was when we first married, I would experience serious marital problems. The love of Christ makes provision for dramatic differences in life and marriage.

Covenant Rhythms

While no man can change a marriage covenant after it has been ratified at the wedding, God can enhance the marriage covenant by revelation of his will for the marriage. To understand this enhancement process, consider the progression from the old covenant to the new covenant. God introduced the old covenant between himself and Israel at Mount Sinai (Exodus 19:3-8). It contained conditions and promises, and it was ratified in a ritualistic service (Exodus 24:4-8). This covenant set a standard for God and man. Then God gave his only begotten son, Jesus, so those who believe in him might have eternal life. Thus he established a new and better covenant based on better promises (Hebrews 8:6). The new covenant is the covenant of the Spirit, which gives new life (2 Corinthians 3:6). It is written on the hearts of the people rather than on stone tablets. This process of covenant enhancement has important implications for the marriage covenant, which is enhanced by God's participation in the marriage.

During each wedding ceremony, the bride and groom exchange vows, which are promises to each other. Like the old covenant introduced at Mount Sinai, these wedding vows become an elementary expression of the marriage covenant and a standard for the husband and wife. When God is welcomed into the marital relationship, he imparts himself into the marriage as a partner with the husband and wife. "God … has invited you into partnership with his Son, Jesus Christ our Lord" (1 Corinthians 1:9b NLT). God gives all of himself to the marriage just like Jesus gave all of himself to establish the new covenant. God is able to give his all for each marriage, because he is an infinite being. The husband and wife can follow his leading and give their all to the marriage. As the Spirit reveals God's will for the marriage, the marriage covenant is enhanced. For example, our wedding vows included the phrase "for better, for worse, for richer, for poorer", but Jesus came to give us an abundant life (John 10:10). We stand on God's promises and refuse to accept less. Our wedding vows also included the phrase "in sickness and in health" but with the word of God we appropriate the healing Jesus purchased for us by the stripes on his back (1 Peter 2:24). We chose to believe the word of God and rejected the doubt and unbelief of traditional wedding vows. We never settle for poverty, lack or sickness.

God's will for the marriage is revealed in rhythmic waves of the Spirit as the husband and wife seek to know more about the eternal purposes for their marriage. The Spirit flows out of the heart of believers like rivers of living water (John 7:38-39). There is no limit on the richness of the marriage, because there is no limit on God. As long as the husband and wife flow with the Spirit in doing God's will, their marriage will remain alive and healthy.

Identifying Three Pillars of Marriage

The marriage covenant is built on three important pillars: spirit of love, intimacy and faith. These three pillars are not static and inflexible. Instead they grow and develop. These pillars stand on a great spiritual wave which follows the Spirit. They move with the Spirit. Marriage without love is cold. Marriage without intimacy is barren. Marriage without faith is sin. These three pillars are addressed in more detail in the next three chapters.

Concluding Remarks

The marriage covenant based on the word of God is alive, because his word is alive. The Spirit brings it to life in the husband and wife who open their heart and mind to seek the Father's will. This living marriage covenant grows without limit inside the husband and wife, touching every aspect of marriage. By walking in this living covenant, married couples can be fruitful, multiply, fill the earth with God's glory and subdue it.

Chapter 5

PILLAR 1: SPIRIT OF LOVE

Love ignites a fire in marriage. Although the term love can take different forms and mean different things, the spirit of love is the highest form of love and the one addressed in this book. God has given believers a spirit of love (2 Timothy 1:7 NKJ). It is God's unconditional love which is spirit. The Spirit floods the hearts of believers with this spirit of love. "The love of God has been poured out within our hearts through the Holy Spirit who was given to us" (Romans 5:5b).

Love is always required in marriage. Even when the husband and wife do not know which scripture relates to a situation, they can always choose the action to express Christ's love. Love fulfills all marriage requirements. "Love does no wrong to a neighbor; therefore love is the fulfillment of the law" (Romans 13:10).

Understanding the Spirit of Love

The spirit of love, which is also called the love of Christ, is far greater than any natural love. The greatest love a person can show is to die for his friends (John 15:13). Jesus' death on the cross is the ultimate expression of this love. When a husband and wife focus on the spirit of love, they will never be without it, regardless of how difficult the situation becomes. Suffering, affliction, tribulation, calamity and distress cannot separate them from the love of Christ (Romans 8:35).

A brief glimpse of Christ's love is provided in 1 Corinthians 13:4-8. These verses describe love by what it is, what it is not and what it will always be.

- Love is patient and kind.
- Love is not jealous, arrogant, self-seeking or record-keeping.
- Love will always believe, hope and endure.

This passage provides fundamental guidelines for love, but it does not encompass everything about love from the word of God.

A rich view of love allowing for growth and change is given in the Song of Songs. This picture of love includes courtship, engagement, marriage and maturity. From its beginnings, the Song describes love as better than wine (Song of Songs 1:2). A person can be intoxicated with a spouse's love (Proverbs 5:19). Through the Song, readers can view their own level of spiritual and emotional growth throughout different stages of life. The bridegroom in this book is Solomon. His name, which is a masculine name for peace, comes from the Hebrew word shalom. The bride in the Song is Shulamite, which is the feminine name derived from shalom. With the names for both lovers being derived from peace, their lives are closely joined together. The Lord will keep in perfect peace those who trust in him (Isaiah 26:3). Hence, the place of God's perfect peace is the ultimate goal of a spiritual marriage.

The Song can be viewed from several perspectives with the readers seeing themselves in the story. First, the Song might be considered as only a sensual love story. This would be fleshly and carnal way to view this story. From another perspective the Song might be viewed as a story about the growth of a relationship between a man and woman who are deeply in love. The relationship progresses through courtship and engagement, then marriage and eventually maturity in life. In this case the bridegroom represents the man and the bride represents the woman. The bride receives from the husband and responds to the husband. Their fire of love bursts into an intense flame, sweeping away everything before it (Song of Songs 8:6). From a deeper spiritual perspective, the Song reflects a spiritual love story. In this case the bridegroom symbolizes Christ, and the bride represents either a particular believer or a body of believers. In the case of a particular believer, the believer (either male or female) receives from Christ and responds to Christ. Receiving from the bridegroom and responding to the bridegroom are consistent with a traditional role of the bride. These are the characteristics a typical bride displays in her relationship with the bridegroom, but she also displays other prominent characteristics while confronting the world. The bridegroom describes his bride like a beautiful city and a fearsome army (Song of Songs 6:4).

The Spirit will establish the husband and wife in love so they will know the breadth, length, height and depth of the love of Christ (Ephesians 3:17-19).The love of Christ is described as having four dimensions, which makes it unlike the things of this world. To help understand this concept, consider the dimensions of things in this world. A map on a piece of paper has only two dimensions. Any point on the map can be found by knowing the length and height from the origin. Adding a third dimension locates any place on the earth. Any location on the earth can be found from these three dimensions. However, there is a fourth dimension of the love of Christ. Natural love cannot approach the fourth dimension of the love of Christ. It cannot be compared with the love of Christ. The natural mind cannot comprehend the love of Christ. The mind of a believer can be renewed to the word of God to see into the love of Christ. The Spirit searches the deep things of God and shows them to us (1 Corinthians 2: 10). Keep your eyes on Jesus Christ, who is your beloved. He is the perfect picture and substance of the groom.

Receiving the Spirit of Love

It is possible to know about the spirit of love without actually receiving this love. It is important to receive love. This section explains how to receive the spirit of love and what can hinder receiving it.

Many things in the world block people from receiving love from heaven. The word of God identifies pride and lust as hindrances to love. "If anyone loves the world, the love of the Father is not in him" (1 John 2:15b). Specific hindrances include lust of the flesh, lust of the eyes and pride of life (1 John 2:16). Lust of the flesh is evident in the cries of the flesh for the things in the world (e.g. cigarettes, alcohol, drugs, sex, power, and success). Lust of the eye relates to those things the world offers (e.g. fame, power, money, faster cars, bigger homes, the latest gadgets and new mates). The pride of life relates to a person thinking it is possible to get all he/she wants on his/her own intelligence, good looks or abilities without relying on God.

In addition to avoiding hindrances, believers have to be prepared to receive the spirit of love. First, it takes knowledge to receive love. This study is aimed at increasing your knowledge of love. Second, humility and crucifying the flesh are needed in preparation for receiving love. "For this reason the Father loves me, because I lay down my life so that I may take it again" (John 10:17). If you lay down your natural life to take up your spiritual life, you are able to receive Christ's life and love (John 12:24).

While Jesus Christ qualifies believers to receive love, they receive love through their relationship with the Father and the work of his Spirit. The Spirit deposits love in a believer's heart. In order to receive more love, spend more time in fellowship with the Lord through praise and prayer. Talk to him and he will talk to you. As believers are filled with the spirit of love, they will desire to fellowship with the Lord, praise him and pray.

Sharing the Spirit of Love with Your Spouse

A husband and a wife can demonstrate the spirit of love to his/her spouse only to the extent to which it has been received. As evidence of your receiving love, you will be obedient to his commands (John 14:31). Jesus gave the one commandment to love like he loves. This commandment is to love one another, as he loved us (John 15:12). Love empowers you to love as Jesus loves you. You will not transgress against your spouse (e.g. adultery, lie, cheat, and steal) if you love him/her.

Be led by the Spirit in all you do. Show your spouse the spirit of love operating through you. As you pour out the spirit of love, you will want to pray for your spouse. Prayer comes straight out of love and pours love onto your spouse.

If you love your spouse, you will speak the word of God and pour out the word of God on him/her. God so loved that he gave his Son, who is the word (John 3:16). Those who want a wonderful marriage will become perfected in their love walk (1 John 2:5; 4:12). Those who are perfected in love will speak the oracles of God to their spouse. They will be hearing the Father's voice which is full of love. Demonstrating the spirit of love will bring freedom and abundance to your marriage.

Personal Story - How Sherry Loves

The Spirit placed within Sherry his supernatural love for all people. For God so loved the world he gave his son (John 3:16). Years ago the Lord said, "Sherry, give yourself to the people." Her immediate response was, "No, Lord, they will kill me." Then after much prayer, she relented and gave herself to the people. He helped her do it. Some have crucified her with their words and actions, but she is still alive and kicking. Sherry is one of his sons, and he has given her to the world to bring reconciliation and deliverance.

Sherry loves the people and freely expresses love, and they love her in return. Every place she goes, people are immediately drawn like a magnet to her. After each time she ministers, the people gather around her to love her, be loved by her and ask for prayer. Recently in Spain, the young people gathered around her between services. Even though they could not communicate with her because of language barriers, they wanted to be near her. At times the crowds around Sherry are so large she has to be rescued to have time to rest and eat.

In a recent letter a woman gave a good explanation about the love people see in Sherry. The woman met Sherry only once a few months earlier as she ministered in another state. She wrote about how Sherry ministered and moved among the people unlike any other person. The woman prayed and asked the Lord, "Why is Sherry different from other people?" The Lord's response was Sherry had love and nothing but love for the people. I know the love of Christ makes Sherry unique and powerful so people everywhere love her and want to be near her.

Concluding Remarks

The spirit of love has to be experienced far it can never be adequately explained with words. Those who have experienced the spirit of love are empowered to love others. They may not be able to explain it very well, but they can express it flawlessly through their actions. It changes their lives and makes them more like Christ. It is an expression of Christ himself. Experiencing his love ignites a fire in the husband and wife which cannot be quenched.

Chapter 6

PILLAR 2: INTIMACY

Intimacy involves a close, affectionate personal relationship. Without intimacy, marriage is barren and unproductive in the kingdom. Love and affection produce a lasting intimacy in marriage. True intimacy, which involves totally sharing oneself with another, is critical for a spiritual marriage. Intimacy is often misunderstood, because it is more than sexual intercourse. It may include sexual intercourse, but sex without affection would not be considered true intimacy.

Understanding the Forms of Intimacy

Intimacy is broader than just sexual intimacy. It can take on several forms.

Sexual intimacy involves meeting each other's sexual needs. In a spiritual marriage, the partners share their full rights with each other. The wife gives authority over her body to the husband, and the husband gives authority over his body to the wife (1 Corinthians 4:7).

Emotional intimacy involves sharing emotional feelings about the relationship and the partners. Emotional intimacy depends on trust. A husband and wife are more likely to share emotional feelings if they trust one another. These feelings are freely shared only if a partner trusts they will be received in a positive way.

Intellectual intimacy involves thoughtful sharing of facts, ideas and philosophies. Shared interests and appreciation for the spouse's viewpoints will enhance a marriage relationship.

Spiritual intimacy involves sharing deep beliefs. The spiritual relationship is the core of a spiritual marriage. It gives meaning and substance to the marriage. God intends for the spiritual relationship to be manifested in every aspect of the marriage. Thus the marriage would be indicative of the unseen spiritual relationship. Sharing beliefs early in a relationship is important, because many believers want to marry someone with a similar faith. "Do not be bound together with unbelievers" (2 Corinthians 6:14a). Sharing beliefs allow the partners to build meaning into the relationship and allow them to grow spiritually as a married couple. This type of sharing helps prepare the couple to fulfill purpose and destiny.

Rhythms of Intimacy

Young girls typically experience sexual awakening earlier than young boy. Then their sexual desire may increase over 15 or 20 years, peeking near the age of 30. In some cultures older men may prefer to marry young girls because they understand their sexual desires and see their potential as partners in marriage over many years. Young boys may become interested in sex later than girls but then their sexual desires typically increase quickly and may peak by the age of 18 to 20. Their sexual desires may remain high for several years. The rhythms of sexual desires of the husband and the wife are generally different. A large difference between what one partner desires in sex and the other provides may cause a partner to turn to someone else to meet their needs, but such behavior is not of the Lord. He is faithful, and he requires faithfulness in others: "But the Lord is faithful, and he will strengthen and protect you from the evil one" (2 Thessalonians 3:3). Flowing in the marriage relationship with the help of the Spirit can improve the intimacy experience.

Intimacy can be a pathway to deep emotions, like passion. Deep emotions are strongly felt and internalized. They may be associated with something of significant value to the individual or some significant event in life. Deep emotions have lasting impacts and can be positive or negative in nature. Vulnerabilities related to deep emotions may be exposed through intimacy. Many partners are fearful of exposing their vulnerabilities and try to block this pathway by limiting intimacy in marriage.

With intimacy releasing deep emotions, marriage becomes an arena in which partners may feel a freedom to express deep emotions. Such freedom may lead to the expression of either positive or negative emotions. There are some constraints on expressing emotions in public settings, such as societal norms and business guidelines. However, a husband or wife may feel no such constrains in expressing deep emotions to his/her spouse. A partner who is carnally minded might express rage or violence towards his/her spouse, even though these things might not be expressed publicly. While there may appear to be no natural constraints in marriages, there are constraints for a husband and wife who walk in the Spirit. Those who fear the Lord are constrained by Christ's love (2 Corinthians 5:11-14). Self-control is included in the fruit of the Spirit (Galatians 5:22-23). "Now those who belong to Christ Jesus have crucified the flesh with its passions and desires" (Galatians 5:24).

The existence of negative emotions in either the husband or wife indicates more things in his/her life need to be resolved and brought under the lordship of the Spirit. It might mean inner healing is needed or the blood of Jesus needs to be applied through faith. Forgiveness is often the most important remedy for such problems. Forgiveness is examined in more detail in chapter 8. Regardless of what the root causes of the problems may be, they need to be addressed. Each partner should try to help the other one deal with root causes of these problems.

Personal Story --Spiritual Intimacy

One of my great enjoyments in life is to spend time with Sherry discussing spiritual things. When we come together to seek the Lord, he always speaks to us by his Spirit. We never take a trip together without asking to hear from the Spirit. When we want to know about something specific, we take a day trip to spend time apart and hear the Spirit. While driving, we always carry pen and paper to write down what the Spirit says. This time together might be called "quality time" in the natural, but to us it is a form of spiritual intimacy. Even though we like visiting new places and doing new things, our most important time together is focused on spiritual things. In these times, the Spirit has revealed things which changed our lives. Such profound truths affect my soul and cause my spirit to soar. Nothing compares to being caught up in the realm of the Spirit and hearing what he says.

Our first book, "Walking in the Father's Riches: Prosperity of Sonship", was a product of spiritual intimacy. Sherry and I began seeking the Lord specifically about his plan for finances and prosperity in 1993. We studied the word and prayed together. The Spirit revealed many truths about these topics. One profound truth we learned was the spirit must first prosper and then the soul prospers and then the body or physical realm prospers. The spirit is the container and when it overflows from the blessings of heaven it will pour into the soul and onto the body or physical realm. Teaching materials were developed and used in different congregations over the next few years. In 2009 the Spirit led us to seek deeper revelation in order to write a book on these topics. Again we spent time together in prayer and study, seeking deeper revelation. The revelation of the Spirit came so quickly the first draft of the book was completed in six weeks.

Some significant things happened between the time we first wrote about these topics and the time we wrote the book. The Lord connected us with significant spiritual relationships. The mature believers in those relationships showed where our thinking was tainted by doctrines of men and how to be freer in the spiritual realm. By the Spirit and by the word, our minds were renewed. By the time we wrote the book, we were prepared better to understand the deep truths about finances and prosperity. Several lessons can be drawn from this experience dealing with spiritual intimacy. Seeking the Lord and praying together help a husband and wife enter spiritual intimacy. Spiritual relationships in the body of Christ can help the married couple grow spiritually and experience rich spiritual intimacy. A husband and wife can experience wonderful things in spiritual intimacy.

Concluding Remarks

While unconditional love can exist where there is no trust, intimacy requires trust. Intimacy exists and flourishes only in relationships built on trust. Without trust a relationship between a man and woman may offer sensual pleasures for a season but not true intimacy. Trust is the heart of intimacy for it nurtures and sustains intimacy. Beauty, strength and intellect will not sustain intimacy for these will fade away. Trust is tested and proven over time. When it endures the tests, it grows stronger and stronger. Trust can be greater at the end than at the beginning. As trust grows, so can intimacy.

Intimacy may take on many different forms over the life of a marriage. At times sexual intimacy may dominate other forms of intimacy, particularly in the early stages of marriage. Other forms of intimacy may become more prominent over time, reflecting more maturity in a marriage. Emotional and intellectual intimacy may seem unimportant early in marriage to a husband and/or wife, but these forms of intimacy can help bring maturity to a marriage. Any hindrances to intimacy in these areas need to be addressed.

Spiritual intimacy, which is missing from many marriages, involves the husband and wife seeking spiritual things together. Such intimacy helps transform a carnal marriage into a spiritual marriage. Spiritual intimacy is critical for the married couple to discover purpose and fulfill destiny together. Otherwise, the husband and wife can only fulfill their individual destinies.

Chapter 7

PILLAR 3: FAITH

Faith is powerful and important in marriage. By faith, a married couple will be able to know God, overcome adversities, and live in abundance. Strong faith is needed to fulfill destiny for a married couple. This section examines three important areas in which faith can be strengthened. It examines how to build faith, purify it and use it to sustain and advance the marriage.

Strengthening faith is a simple process, because children can have strong faith. However, the process is best accomplished with an action plan like gathering evidence of the unseen world, purging doubt and applying faith. Building strong faith takes time and persistence. Do not wait until you face the enemy in a great battle to begin strengthening your faith. Now is the time to build and purify your faith and use it to fight evil for yourself and for your spouse.

Gather Evidence to Build Faith

Faith is evidence from the unseen world. "Now faith is the substance of things hoped for, the evidence of things not seen" (Hebrews 11:1 KJV). Faith comes from the anointed word of God. Every time the Spirit speaks God's word to believers or brings a scripture to life for them, the amount of their evidence from the unseen world increases. The more evidence believers gather, the stronger their faith becomes. Gathering knowledge about God without experiencing him creates strong religious opinions: knowledge makes people boastful (1 Corinthians 8:1). However, their religious opinions about God and the operation of faith do not build strong faith.

The following two examples of people with great faith show a direct connection between the word of God and strong faith. The centurion, who wanted Jesus to speak the word so his servant would be healed, had great faith (Matthew 8:8-10). He recognized authority and submitted to the authority of God's word as spoken by Jesus. The mother of a demon-possessed girl, who acknowledged the words of Jesus as being the truth, had great faith (Matthew 15:22-28). Submitting to the authority of God's word will strengthen your faith.

Purge Doubt to Purify Faith

Doubt comes from not knowing the truth about God's word but believing lies which distort the truth. Doubt in any area of a person's life will contaminate all areas. A little leaven in bread dough leavens or spreads throughout the whole lump of dough (Galatians 5:9). Purge out the old leaven so you can be a new lump (1 Corinthians 5:7). In order for a believer to have strong faith all doubt has to be eliminated. Jesus taught if a person has faith and not any doubt, then his/her faith will move mountains (Matthew 21:21 and Mark 11:23). A mixture of faith and doubt is weak faith at best.

Believers face a struggle within between the carnal mind (flesh) and the spirit of man. The carnal mind opposes the things of God, while the spirit of man agrees with God. Believers are taught to put off the old man (carnal mind) and put on the new man (spirit) (Ephesians 4:22-24). A good way to help understand this struggle is to compare it to a spinning coin, which is white on one side and black on the other. As long as the white side of the coin is on top, the spirit of man rules over darkness. Whenever the coin flips over with the black side on top, the carnal mind dominates the person. Consider an example of how the coin can flip over, showing two different natures in the same believer. While a believer is communing with the Lord, studying the word of God and/or meditating on the things of God, the white side of the coin is on top. However, whenever the spouse or children aggravate the same believer, the coin could flip over and expose the dark side through anger or other negative emotions. This concept of a spinning coin can help explain where doubt resides and how to deal with doubt. All doubt resides on the dark side. All faith resides on the light side for the word of God which produces faith is light. "Your word is a lamp to my feet and a light to my path" (Psalm 119:105). A believer can pursue the things of God and add to the light side of the coin. However, these actions do not negate doubt residing on the dark side. Doubt can be purged from the dark side by identifying it and applying the blood of Jesus to it. His blood purges doubt and cleanses the conscience (Hebrews 9:14). Doubt can also be eliminated by speaking the word of truth.

Fight for the Marriage with Faith

While building faith and purifying faith, believers can begin to put faith to work. Exercising faith strengthens it. James wrote "faith without works is dead" (James 2:20). These works are not just performance like attending church services and singing songs, but they are actions relating directly to what the person believes. In healing crusades Oral Roberts told the people whom he prayed for to do something they could not do beforehand. Some paralyzed people began to walk even when it was a struggle at first. These actions related directly to what they believed, strengthening their faith. Some could just blink their eyes and then suddenly felt the power of God come into their bodies and heal them.

Centering a marriage on Christ strengthens the faith of the husband and wife. Christ becomes the center of a marriage as they receive the anointed word of God and renew their minds. The Spirit plays an important role in renewing their minds by revealing the word. A person can acquire intellectual knowledge about the word without relying on the Spirit, but his/her mind is not renewed. As the Spirit reveals the word and brings it to life, faith for the marriage arises in the husband and wife. They will have faith to appropriate the promises of God for the marriage. Although confessing the word without hearing from the Spirit is an empty gesture, confessing what the Spirit has spoken releases faith and brings forth much power.

There is a war going on between the forces of good and evil. Faith fights spiritually from a position of victory not simply for victory. Using faith in the battle strengthens it. Smith Wigglesworth said great faith comes out of great battles. The battle does not strengthen faith but using faith in the midst of battle strengthens it. The real battle in marriage is not between the husband and wife but against spiritual forces of evil. "Our struggle is not against flesh and blood, but against the rulers, against the powers, against the world forces of this darkness, against the spiritual forces of wickedness in the heavenly places" (Ephesians 6:12). Recognizing your spouse is not the enemy will help you be able to stand in the midst of battle. As a husband and wife operate in unison to overcome difficulties their strength is multiplied. One can put a thousand enemies to flight but two can put ten thousand to flight (Deuteronomy 32:30). God gives believers many spiritual weapons to fight the battles (2 Corinthians 10:4). Hold up faith as a shield to stop the enemy. All of the spiritual weapons operate effectively with faith.

Take pleasure in the smallest victories. They are the flavor and appetizer for more victories to come. Even a deluge of rainfall to end a drought begins with the first drop of rain. I like to thank the Lord for every drop of rain. Financial independence may start with one bill being paid. Healing in your body may start with a small decrease in your body's temperature. Note every victory. Do not let the victories go unnoticed, because any one of them could be a critical victory turning the tide of the war. Such victories are part of the believer's evidence from the unseen world.

Personal Story ‑ Fighting with Faith

Over 20 years ago, Sherry began to have health problems. We prayed and sought medical help for the problems. As I prayed for her on December 2, 1992, the Spirit of God said, "We have the victory over this thing." I began to thank the Lord for this promise and marked the spot by drawing an invisible "X" on the floor with my foot to remember it. For several days we thanked the Lord and stood on his promise.

Four weeks later, Sherry received a telephone call from the doctor who gave her a bad report. She drove through the neighborhood looking for me. I was walking and praying for her. When I got into the car, she said three doctors agreed she had cancer and was expected to live only six months. Like the Spirit said earlier, I told her "We have the victory over this thing." I immediately told her to pack the bags, because we were going to take a trip to shut out the world and to hear from the Spirit. It was our way of keeping our faith strong in the face of such devastating news. We spent time together in prayer, believing for a miracle in her body. During the trip the Spirit encouraged our faith, letting us know we could trust him to take care of this situation.

In the first week of January 1993, I began teaching a six-week session on healing. I started the session by telling the people Sherry had been diagnosed with cancer, and then I declared she would stand and proclaim her healing before the end of the six weeks. As I was teaching the word on healing, the Spirit came upon Sherry, pouring hot oil over her. She was supernaturally lifted off the seat. Later in the week she underwent exploratory surgery, but the doctors could find no cancer. The doctor said somebody had removed the cancer before the surgery. Before I taught the second lesson on healing, Sherry stood and proclaimed she had been healed as the Lord promised.

Concluding Remarks

Faith never settles for less than God's best. Faith is continually moving and acting for if it ever stops it dies. Faith without action is dead. Those who are satisfied in their situation are not operating in faith; they might talk faith but not be in faith. Faith is an issue of the heart. When operating in faith, a person's heart does not accuse him/her before God.

Faith operates in marriage when the hearts of the husband and wife are united. Verbal agreement alone is not the same as being in faith. Nothing is beyond the reach of a husband and wife who operate in faith. The Father himself will give them what they desire. They are invincible.

Chapter 8
MENDING PILLARS: FORGIVENESS
AND BLESSINGS

A marriage partner's words or actions can wound the other partner. Such wounds can have serious ramifications, even damaging the three pillars of marriage, if not dealt with quickly. A wounded spirit cannot overcome adversity as well as a strong and healthy spirit (Proverbs 18:14). Unforgiveness is selfish. It covers the wounds and keeps them from being healed. Several negative emotions, such as envy, strife, resentment, anger and bitterness, can arise from the wound. A root of bitterness can grow up in a marriage partner because of unforgiveness. This root can be buried deep inside the person and can block the flow of Christ's love from penetrating deep into the heart. It can also block the flow of the Spirit through a partner. Confessing and forsaking unforgiveness, as well as other sins, releases God's mercy to heal the wound (Proverbs 28:13). It helps to forgive someone and then bless that person will a blessing to solidify the forgiveness. This chapter addresses both forgiveness and blessings.

Forgiveness

Forgiveness in marriage is patterned after the Father's forgiveness. Forgive as your Father has forgiven you. It takes the Spirit to enable believers to forgive just as the Father forgives. Any unforgiveness is bondage which is accompanied by all manner of negative emotions. Nothing good comes from any bondage. Forgiveness releases both you and your spouse from the bondage of unforgiveness. Let the Spirit help you to forgive so your spirit can be set free.

Pray to Forgive your Spouse

Pray for your spouse when you have been hurt. Approach the throne of grace and petition your Father in heaven to forgive him/her. Ask your Father to pour out grace, mercy, and compassion upon him/her. Name every sin and wrong committed against you. The Spirit will reveal them to you so they can be covered by the blood of Jesus.

Ask your Father in the name of Jesus and by the blood Jesus shed on the cross to forgive each sin which has been committed against you. As you name each sin against you and ask your Father to forgive, then your burdens will be rolled away.

Forgive by Faith

Forgive, because the word of God teaches forgiveness (Matthew 6:14). Jesus saw the faith of the paralyzed man and his friends who carried him up on the roof to be healed. Jesus dealt with the paralyzed man's sins before he healed him (Mark 2:5-11). Forgive first by faith and then be made whole. The blood of Jesus makes your conscience pure, taking away even the memory of hurts (Hebrews 9:14). Sometimes, we instruct people to write down who they want to forgive and then throw away the paper. A simple deed like this can help activate faith for forgiveness. Even if it takes time for negative emotions to leave, they can remember the paper and the time they activated faith rather than remembering the hurt.

Forgive your Spouse Often

The more you are wronged, the more you are to forgive. There is no limit on forgiveness. Peter thought surely seven times would be the maximum number of times to forgive someone. However, Jesus said to forgive seventy times seven (Matthew 18:21 22). Be quick to forgive your spouse.

Forgive to Eliminate the Debt against your Spouse

When you forgive the debt your spouse owes you, then he/she no longer has a negative balance in your records. Instead, the negative balance is wiped away and converted to a zero balance. In other words, the balance owed you becomes neither positive nor negative. "The lord of that slave felt compassion and released him and forgave him the debt" (Matthew 18:22-27).

Blessings

God forgave us, and he blessed us. After our huge debt was completely wiped away, we had a zero balance in God's records. However, he did not leave us with a zero balance. He blessed us with all spiritual blessings in Christ Jesus (Ephesians 1:3). He has granted to us everything pertaining to life and godliness (2 Peter 1:3). When he sees you, he does not think about your sins which have been blotted out (Colossians 3:14). Instead, the Father thinks about the investment he made in you, which includes the blood of Jesus, all spiritual blessings and everything pertaining to life and godliness.

The carnal mind (fleshly thinking) wants revenge. It says, "An eye for an eye, and a tooth for a tooth. Hate your enemies. Curse those who curse you. Render evil for evil." But Jesus said love your enemies and pray for those who persecute you, so you may be like your Father who is in heaven (Matthew 5:43 45). If you have the attitude, faith, and prayer life of Jesus Christ, you will bless your spouse even though he/she has wronged you. "Bless those who persecute you; bless and do not curse" (Romans 12:14).

Hosea offers a great example of blessing a spouse (Hosea 3:1-3). Hosea's wife deserted him for an adulterous affair with another man. He went to her and gave her instructions on how to live until she could be restored as his wife. "You shall not play the harlot, nor shall you have a man; so I will also be toward you" (Hosea 3:3). He also gave her silver and grain to live on until her full restoration. Having given a gift to his wife, Hosea had something to remember other than the wife's unfaithfulness.

After blessing your spouse you will remember the blessing rather than the wrong he/she committed. There will be no negative emotions associated with the blessing. Hence the negative emotions, which may have tormented you while you walked in unforgiveness, would be eliminated with forgiveness and blessings. When you think about your spouse, you will remember the blessing. You will walk in the Spirit and in peace.

Personal Story - Offenses, Forgiveness and Gift Giving

Sherry is quick to rise in defense of family members and loved ones. Many people ask her to pray for them, because they know she is a person of faith who takes things seriously. She prays earnestly. When someone hurts anyone close to her, she is affected and sometimes takes up an offense about another person's pain. Taking up an offense is not good. When the Spirit deals with her heart about the offense, she repents and forgives the person. However, she does not stop at forgiveness, because she loves giving gifts and receiving gifts. Frequently, she gives a gift to a person who has committed an offense. This act of gift giving helps her stay free from offenses and unforgiveness, because she chooses to remember the gift she gave rather than the offense.

Concluding Remarks

A married couple needs to know how to protect the marriage from the schemes of the devil. Marriages are targeted by the enemy for destruction. Strife is one of the main tools used against a marriage. It feeds on unfaithfulness and unforgiveness. Unforgiveness attached to a single act of unfaithfulness often escalates to open hostility in marriage. Someone has to recognize what is going on in the marriage and respond to correct problems. Many times, a couple must be delivered from past events and hurts in order to focus on the future. Repentance and forgiveness give a married couple immediate relief.

Chapter 9
POPULAR VIEWS OF MARRIAGE

For the best results, approach marriage with a well-conceived and deliberate plan. One of the most basic issues in planning a marriage relates to the form of marriage to pursue. Many people approach marriage as an extension of the lives they have already chosen. Before marriage they made major decisions concerning life, especially their relationship with God. Typically, marriage is approached as just the next step on the path of life already chosen. People with a natural or worldly approach to life would probably pursue a natural marriage. Carnal people, who have God living in them but resist having his power work through them, would probably pursue a carnal marriage. Many in both of these groups do not understand the form of marriage chosen or the consequences of their choices. The discussions in this chapter on worldly and carnal marriages and the next chapter on spiritual marriages are intended to help people make good choices about which form of marriage to pursue. Even though Sherry and I recommend a spiritual marriage for all, some couples may not be ready for a spiritual marriage. This chapter identifies the two most popular forms of marriage and addresses the consequences of these forms of marriage.

Worldly View of Romance and Marriage

The first type of marriage, which is called a worldly or natural marriage, focuses on romance, affection and attention without involving God. This relates to the media's perfect marriage. Movies and romance novels provide a picture of this type of marriage. The husband remembers the wife's birthday, their anniversary, and special occasions and provides gifts, flowers and fine dining. The wife may arrange for candle-lit dinners for her and her husband and for special get-away trips for the two of them. Even when children come along, the married couple can make arrangements for special times together, such as travel and dates to eat at a fine restaurant, walk and talk in the park and go to a movie.

Inherent Problems with Worldly Marriages

Romance does not adequately prepare couples for the difficulties they may face through the years of married life. How will they deal with problems related to careers, finances, sex, children, and extended family? What happens when the flame of passion for each other flickers and fades? Nothing in the worldly marriage permanently connects the married couple together. If someone who is more romantic, affectionate or attentive comes along, then one of the partners may abandon the relationship.

A worldly marriage is based on emotions and other natural forces, because the spirits of the husband and wife have not been regenerated. A person must be regenerated by the Spirit to see spiritual things (John 3:3-6). Manipulation and control problems are evident in worldly marriages, because these relationships are based on emotions and other natural things. The husband and wife are not under spiritual authority, so they are on their own in making decisions. If the husband abuses and mistreats the wife, she might accept abuse, seek a safe refuge, counsel or help from police or even pursue divorce. Most of these options do not address the root causes of marital problems. Attempts to correct major problems without dealing with root causes will be ineffective.

A worldly marriage does not rely on God. It is temporal in nature and subject to change at any time. Love in the worldly marriage is a natural or conditional love. As long as the wife does everything to please the husband, he loves her. However, if her body, mind, words, behavior or actions are not pleasing to the husband, his love for her could diminish. Likewise, the wife's love for the husband could diminish if something about him is not pleasing to her.

Assessment of the Worldly Marriage

Even with a well-planned worldly marriage, the couple may face marital problems related to sex, finances, in-laws, careers, parenting, etc. The couple may seek counsel from friends and relatives, see a marriage counselor or read self-help books on marriage. Many people are willing to share practical advice for improving these marriages. The advice of others would be based on their experiences of what worked and what did not work in their own lives, as well as knowledge obtained from other sources. Such information may or may not be appropriate for the specific problems faced by other couples. The only one who can help resolve every marital problem is the Lord, but those in worldly marriages tend to reject his help. Even with all of the available information on how to have a successful marriage, half of the worldly marriages end in divorce. Worldly marriages often face unresolved problems, not apparent to outsiders. Some worldly marriages avoiding divorce may not be considered as successful by the husband and wife themselves.

Carnal View of Love and Marriage

The second type of marriage, which is prevalent among Christians, is based on a core of biblical teachings. Typically, the core concepts are not explicitly identified and may vary from one married couple to another. A few similar concepts would be expected in many of these marriages. For example, the husband loves his wife and the wife respects her husband (Ephesians 5:33).

The idea of some core concepts may seem reasonable, and most Christian couples claim they abide by such concepts. However, keeping traditional biblical concepts through a person's own natural abilities is carnal behavior, and a marriage based on this approach can be called a carnal marriage. Carnality is fleshly in nature and characterized by jealousy and strife (1 Corinthians 3:1-3).

Inherent Problems with Carnal Marriages

People cannot keep God's commandments in their own natural strength, so he sent a savior. If they transgress any commandment, they are guilty of transgressing the whole law. "For whoever keeps the whole law and yet stumbles in one point, he has become guilty of all" (James 2:10). Every marriage needs a savior, and the only possibility for true salvation is through Jesus. A few ramifications of failing to keep God's marriage covenant as God intends are discussed below.

A Form of Godliness without Life: Obeying the basic commandments of God does not ensure an abundant life for marriage. A rich, young ruler asked Jesus how he could receive eternal life (Mark 10:17 22). He claimed he kept all the commandments of God. He wanted to tap into God's life to make up for what was lacking in his own life. Keeping these basic commandments did not ensure he would be able to live the abundant life Jesus promised (John 10:10). Just obeying the basic commandments of God does not ensure a successful life or a successful marriage. A successful marriage is dependent on both partners fulfilling God's plan for their lives and marriage.

Misunderstandings about the Spirit of Love: There are problems with the practice of some biblical concepts related to marriage. Those concepts meant to be standards and hence static pictures of believers in maturity have to be kept in context. An immature believer may misuse these standards trying to force them on his/her spouse. Many believers are not properly equipped for godly marriage without help from mature believers. God's plan for maturity involves teaching both men and women about love (Titus 2:1-6). Both the old and young are to be taught about love. How can believers truly love their spouse if they are never taught how to love like Christ loves? God's plan for maturity involves connecting young men and women with mature believers to instruct them. Young married couples are to be taught how to manage the affairs of life before being able to walk in true abundance (Galatians 4:1-2). However, many young people think they can have a successful marriage without help from anyone. When ministers do not address the process of maturity, they simply show a static image of what the marriage should be. This approach is often frustrating and harmful to young couples who get lost in the process.

Misunderstandings about God's Authority: Another problem encountered by couples who desire a biblical marriage relates to authority and submission. The biblical standard is for the husband to be the head of the wife (Ephesians 5:23) and the wife to submit to her husband (Ephesians 5:22). A problem is evident when an immature husband tries to be a dominating head without submitting to any authority himself. The word of God warns against putting a novice or an immature person into a position of authority (1 Timothy 3:6). This warning applies to marriages, as well as the church. Forcing a wife to submit to an immature husband who does not portray the character of Christ is out of God's order. Although such marriages appear on the surface to be consistent with biblical concepts, they may violate other important concepts. A wife needs to know she can trust her husband as a caring, loving and mature believer.

An Assessment of Carnal Marriages

Although the carnal marriage applies certain concepts from the Bible, it does not truly reflect everything the Bible says about marriage. Instead, scriptures may be applied out of context and without full understanding to create a male-dominated marriage. In such cases, the wife may be forced into submission.

Married couples who try to follow carnal concepts for marriage often face many problems. If they try to resolve these problems, they may turn to ministers, counselors or books on marriage. The problems are often not resolved, because half of these marriages end in divorce. Sadly, the divorce rate among married couples in the church is about the same as among worldly marriages.

Many couples in carnal marriages who do not divorce continue to face major problems in marriage because of inadequate support from mature believers. Christian instruction and literature do not improve married life when the concepts are cold, bankrupt and sterile, missing the abundant life which Jesus promised.

Concluding Remarks

There are some fundamental problems with the two most popular forms of marriage. Such problems are inherent in any human endeavor not Christ-centered and Spirit-led. These problems lead to divorce in half of the worldly marriages and half of the carnal marriages. Even though many natural and carnal marriages do not end in divorce, they still encounter serious unresolved problems. Marriage counselling and teachings relying on anything other than the guidance and empowerment of the Spirit cannot resolve the fundamental problems with worldly and carnal marriages. It takes the Spirit to lead any married couple along the invisible pathway of God's righteousness and through the storms of life. Only the power of the Spirit enables a married couple to be victorious over every situation.

Chapter 10
EVALUATION OF
THE SPIRITUAL MARRIAGE

This chapter examines the concept of a spiritual marriage in detail and provides an assessment of it. A spiritual marriage merges two destinies – the destiny of the husband with the destiny of the wife. Their purposes were first birthed in the heart of God before time began. Initially, only God knows these purposes, but he reveals them to his children by his Spirit (1 Corinthians 2:10). As a husband and wife discover purpose, they can fulfill destiny together. Relationships with the Spirit and mature believers help them discover purpose and fulfill destiny.

A man and woman may begin the discovery process before they are married. For example, each person may understand God's calling on his/her life before marriage. However, the fullness of the man's purpose and the fullness of the woman's purpose are revealed throughout their lifetime. The purpose of the married couple is revealed as the husband and wife mature both individually and as a married couple. In the spiritual marriage, the husband and the wife truly become one – one in the flesh and one in the spirit. They think and act as one, no longer operating as if they were separate

Oneness in Flesh and Spirit

In the Garden of Eden, God created the first human being as both male and female (Genesis 1:27). Before God took the woman out of man, they were one in every respect (Genesis 2:23). God gave them a purpose for existing. They had no other purpose than what God said to them. "Be fruitful and multiply, and fill the earth, and subdue it; and rule over the fish of the sea and over the birds of the sky and over every living thing that moves on the earth" (Genesis 1:28). The union of Adam and Eve before the woman was taken out of the man represents a spiritual marriage in which the man and woman were merged into one being and had forsaken any selfish interests to fulfill God's purpose. From God's perspective, destiny relates to being one with his purpose. Oneness does not relate to individual purpose, but it relates to the purpose and plan of God. God's destiny for each married couple involves the couple being one with his purpose. After the woman was taken out of the man, the man and woman were united in a natural marriage in which they became one flesh (Genesis 2:24). In today's spiritual marriage, the husband and wife are to become one in flesh (Matthew 19:5; Ephesians 5:31) and one in spirit (1 Corinthians 6:17; Philippians 1:27). Unity and agreement for a married couple are powerful, but oneness is greater than both unity and agreement. It takes the glory of God to produce oneness (John 17:22). Oneness is the order God has set forth for the world to see. Only in oneness will the glory of God be manifested. The married couple can achieve oneness when the two of them are of one mind and one accord. "Fill up and complete my joy by living in harmony and being of the same mind and one in purpose, having the same love, being in full accord and of one harmonious mind and intention" (Philippians 2:2 AMP)

In merging destinies, the wife does not give up her identity and merge into the husband. Neither does the husband give up his identity and merge into the wife. Instead, both the husband and wife merge into the Lord, which is truly oneness. Considering the Lord is one with the heavenly Father, merging into the Lord also means merging into the Father. When believers are one with the Father, the Son and each other, then the people of the world will believe the Father sent the Son (John 17:21). A married couple portraying Jesus to their world will have great impact on the people around them.

While the carnal marriage is legalistic in nature and under the law, the spiritual marriage is under grace. The Apostle Paul equated grace with the power of Christ: "My grace is sufficient for you, for power is perfected in weakness" (2 Corinthians 12:9) Like an explosive power, grace propels a married couple into the supernatural realm where they see the invisible Jesus. Moses was able to endure many difficulties in Egypt and the wilderness seeing the one who is invisible (Hebrews 11:27). By grace, a marriage endures as the husband and wife keep their eyes on Jesus.

Growing Together

When a husband and wife are first married, they may be immature in some areas. An immature husband lacks spiritual authority even though he may be destined to operate in much authority. Initially, his decisions may not appear prudent. There may be good reasons for a wife to be concerned about submitting to an immature husband. In order for the wife to have confidence in her husband's decisions, he needs to consistently make decisions she considers to be good ones. It takes time to establish trust in a person's ability to make good decisions. There is a dynamic process by which the husband and wife grow from immaturity to maturity.

In order for the husband and wife to grow spiritually, they need to find their appointed place in the body of Christ. God sets believers in the body as it pleases him (1 Corinthians 12:18). When a husband and wife are joined to mature believers as the Spirit directs and submitted to authority, there is a nurturing and safe environment for the married couple to grow. If the couple is under spiritual authority, the wife will be able to appeal to someone in authority for those decisions her husband makes with which she does not agree. A mature person in authority would assess the situation and help redirect decisions and actions as needed.

No one can fulfill God's destiny on his/her own. Everyone needs anointed ministers of God and mature believers in his/her life. Spiritual relationships help identify and fulfill destiny. Jesus Christ gave the fivefold ministry gifts – apostles, prophets, evangelists, pastors and teachers – to mature and equip the saints so they can fulfill destiny (Ephesians 4:11-12). In particular, a spiritual father can impart life and spiritual gifts into a husband and wife so they may be firmly established (Romans 1:11). Developing close relationships with God's fivefold ministers are very important for married couples.

Prayer helps identify and fulfill destiny. It is possible for a young married couple to have a spiritual marriage from the beginning. In this case, prayer for the marriage partner would begin long before his/her identity is known. Then the couple would begin to pray together earnestly and continually before and after the wedding. Earnest prayers make God's supernatural power available to propel the couple into destiny (James 5:16). These early prayers will help set the course for a spiritual marriage.

Even if the husband and wife do not start off seeking God, they can develop a spiritual marriage later as the Spirit leads. If a married couple starts off in a strictly carnal marriage, they can still turn it around. If carnality, selfishness and ignorance have resulted in deep wounds being inflicted in each other, healing will be needed in order for the couple to develop a spiritual marriage. Repentance for carnality, selfishness and ignorance followed by prayer for cleansing will bring healing for the birthing of a spiritual marriage. The Lord will forgive the sins of the husband and wife and heal their marriage if they humble themselves, pray, seek the Lord and turn from their wicked ways (2 Chronicles 7:14). Prayer is critical for setting a supernatural environment for marriage.

In a spiritual marriage, the husband and wife cover each other with the armor of God as they pray for each other. They also strengthen each other through prayer. They can approach prayer together like the disciples prayed together in the in the book of Acts. The disciples came together to pray when they faced adversity or needed decisions. For example, they prayed for guidance with appropriate references to the scriptures and waited for the Spirit to respond (Acts 4:23-31 and 13:2-3). By praying together, a married couple can discover God's plan for destiny as they hear God's voice and know his heart. By choosing to follow the Lord's plan for the marriage, they can fulfill destiny. Prayer positions the married couple in God's perfect will to fulfill destiny.

Fulfilling the Plan of the Father

Flowing out of the Father's great love is a wonderful plan for each married couple whom he has joined together. "In Christ Jesus, God made [created] us to do good works, which God planned in advance for us to live our lives doing" (Ephesians 2:10 EXB). His good works for the married couple were planned beforehand. To fulfill the plan, the couple must take paths which he prepared ahead of time. By following the paths he prepared and doing the works he planned, the married couple becomes the Father's work of art. A spiritual marriage is a work of art.

His plan for the couple reflects the marriage between Christ and his bride, which is the body of Christ. His plan for the marriage is different from anything the man and woman could plan by themselves. Also, his plan is far better than anything they could imagine on their own. Following the Father's plan for each marriage will accomplish his eternal purposes and fulfill destiny for the married couple. The only way for the Father's plan to be revealed to a married couple is for both of them to have strong personal relationships with the Father, his Son and his Spirit.

The Spirit is the guide to the Father's plan. This plan for each marriage is not written on paper or tablets of stone. Instead, the plan is revealed from heaven by the Spirit (Luke 2:26; 1 Corinthians 2:10). The only way to understand the Father's plan is by revelation of the Spirit. The Spirit is given to believers to reveal God's plan for them. By developing a strong relationship with the Spirit and learning to recognize his voice, each married couple can receive a revelation of the Father's plan for the marriage. The Spirit will show the couple things to come in the future (John 16:13) and lead them into the fullness of God's plan for their individual destinies and for the destiny of their marriage. Obedience to the Father's plan is the highest form of obedience. Obedience to the Father's plan will yield peace, prosperity and success.

Strengths of the Spiritual Marriage

Those couples who actively pursue a spiritual marriage have strong relationships with the Father, his Son and his Spirit. They seek the kingdom of God and his righteousness before anything else, even their own interests (Matthew 6:33). They are motivated by love in everything they do, live by the faith of the Son of God, and walk in the spirit by seeing the invisible.

The husband and wife in a spiritual marriage esteem the other higher than himself/herself. They faithfully guard each other with prayers. They value the marriage relationship above all others and aggressively pursue fulfillment of their joint destinies. They help build up each other.

They have the tools (e.g. love, faith, wisdom, authority, and support) to fight against all the things coming against their lives and marriage. By following the Father's plan for their marriage, they have all of their needs met by Christ Jesus (Philippians 4:19).

Personal Story - Transforming Our Marriage

Sherry and I went through all three types of marriage at different times. First, our marriage started as a worldly marriage based on love, affection and attention. We knew very little about marriage other than what we had observed with our parents. We greatly enjoyed our time together and built a close relationship. However, there was much to be learned about marriage and life together. Open communication was critical during this time to learn from mistakes and move forward.

Second, our marriage shifted more towards a carnal marriage as we began to develop personal relationships with the Lord. The word of God and life with other believers became more important to us during this period of time. We talked about marriage, visited with other couples who were experiencing similar marital problems and studied about marriage. In particular, we studied about the concept of agreement in marriage and tried to be in agreement in all things concerning our marriage. We were filled with the Spirit and walked by faith. We thought a lot of progress had been made in our relationship together. As the Spirit began to reveal the Father's plan for marriage, he changed the way we were thinking and prepared us for a deeper walk in the Spirit.

Third, the Lord began to reveal the concept of a spiritual marriage to us by his Spirit, and we responded to the leading of the Spirit to walk in the Spirit and operate as one in a spiritual marriage. Two critical components were needed for us to operate in a spiritual marriage. First, both of our relationships with the Spirit grew closer and stronger. Second, the Lord joined us with mature believers who helped mature and equip us. No longer were we just exchanging opinions about marriage with other immature married couples facing the same problems we were. Instead, our conversations with mature believers focused on life in the kingdom of God. We matured enough to hear from the Spirit and be led by the Spirit. Our understanding of a spiritual marriage came from no man but by revelation of the Spirit.

Our worldly marriage had been good, our carnal marriage was better, but our spiritual marriage is by far the best. If our marriage had not progressed beyond a carnal marriage, this book would never have been written, because we had nothing to add to the conversation on marriage. Revelation of the spiritual marriage changed our thinking and prompted us to write this book. We learned important things about marriage from the Spirit. Applying these spiritual concepts would have been helpful early in our marriage. This book explains the things about marriage we consider to be most important.

Concluding Remarks

Although the stars have been set in place and the mountains have been formed, the Father's true art is being portrayed by his family fulfilling his plan. A spiritual marriage is the Father's art work. As the husband and wife walk along the paths the Father prepared for them ahead of time and do the works predestined for them, they show forth his glorious handwork. They look like Christ and act like Christ. They are invincible.

At first, married couples may enjoy a honeymoon period in which the partners devote attention to each other. Pressures from the outside world seem to be left behind for the honeymoon, allowing the partners to begin their married life together in joy and peace. Regrettably, the honeymoon does not last long. The honeymoon is said to end when arguments begin. Arguments in marriage may come as a surprise to many, but there are some fundamental reasons for conflicts in marriage. Many couples are not equipped to handle marital problems. They lack important knowledge and key tools to deal with such problems. Understanding root causes of conflicts and tools to deal with these conflicts can help resolve marital problems. This chapter explains how to understand and correct many marital problems. The specific objectives are to: (1) provide knowledge on root causes of marital problems and (2) offer problem-solving tools for marriage.

One Flesh

The foundation for marriage rests in Creation. After God created man and woman, he decreed marriage. "For this reason a man shall leave his father and his mother, and be joined to his wife; and they shall become one flesh" (Genesis 2:24). This verse encompasses three important elements. First, God is the one who ordained marriage, making it holy for he is holy. Second, the family unit is identified as the source from which the man and woman spring forth to enter marriage. The reference to father and mother reflects God's will for family. The family unit is important to God. Third, the man and woman become one flesh through the marriage union. The apostle Paul explained a man and woman would become one flesh through sexual union. Anyone who is joined with a prostitute becomes one with her; "the two will become one" (1 Corinthians 6:16). Many people think the consequences of sexual immorality are no worse than the consequences of eating unhealthy food, but Paul explained a single act of sexual immorality has both dark and long-lasting consequences. When Jesus taught on marriage in the New Testament, he used the original reference to marriage as defined in Creation. "Have you not read that he who created them from the beginning made them male and female, and said, 'For this reason a man shall leave his father and mother and be joined to his wife, and the two shall become one flesh'?" (Matthew 19:4-5) By referring to the original decree, Jesus showed there had been no change in God's original intent and plan for marriage.

Root Causes of Marital Conflict

Although it is easy for a married couple to become one flesh, it is harder to go beyond this level. Root causes of marital conflict have to be addressed to move forward. Three roots are discussed below.

Carnal Goals

When a man and woman wed, they bring different goals into the marriage. Some of these goals relate to their experiences as they were growing up, previous relationships, media, etc. These goals are not static but change through the life of the marriage. With the husband and wife having different goals about marriage, there will be disagreements over how the marriage should function. These disagreements may surface quickly and frequently. When big differences in the goals exist, envy and strife result. One or both of the partners may be envious over power and control in some areas of the marriage. Envy and strife may be suppressed for a period of time but could surface at any moment if the root causes are not corrected.

A married couple can never reach a stable agreement based on carnality or carnal goals. The carnal mind (man's thinking) is hostile against God (Romans 8:7). Carnal thinking produces division in marriage. From the perspective of believers, carnal goals are the wrong goals to pursue, because they involve fleshly pleasures which are hostile to God. It is important to discover God's purpose for a marriage and pursue purpose rather than carnal goals.

Self-interests

How strongly the husband and wife hold onto their goals depends on their own self-interests. Those who are not following the Spirit are controlled by their own selfish desires (1 Corinthians 3:1-3). Self-interests hinder movement towards agreement, because they result in envy and strife rather than harmony. For example, conflict could result from a husband wanting to take the lead in some of the same areas in which the wife wants to take the lead.

Fear of Losing Control

The carnal person wants to be in control, but the spirit man trusts the Father will work out all things for his good pleasure (Romans 8:28). Differences in goals may be resolved by a husband and wife giving up self-interests or yielding some of their perceived rights. They would be reluctant to yield their rights when they are fearful of losing something. The husband may fear losing control if he gives up something for his wife's sake. Likewise, the wife may fear losing identity if she gives up something for her husband's sake. Self-interests and related fears are involved with the root causes for marital strife. Out of self-interests arise "envy, strife, abusive language, evil suspicions, and constant friction" (1 Timothy 6:4-5). In addition to these natural problems, marital disagreements result in serious spiritual problems. For example, prayers are hindered when a husband does not honor his wife (1 Peter 3:7).

Personal Story - A Root Cause of Marital Conflict

A problem in our marriage existed for years without coming to the surface. Sherry took an offense against my dad for the way he treated my mother whom Sherry loved. Even after my dad passed away, she was still angry about what he did. Since I walked and talked like my dad, her anger against him often surfaced against me. Some specific behaviors I exhibited caused immediate reactions from Sherry. She was not aware of the root cause of this problem. When we were trying to resolve our marital problems, the Spirit exposed this deep root. She forgave my dad and the anger issue was resolved. Many lessons can be learned from this experience. The root of anger has to be dealt with or it will surface in unexpected ways for years. Unforgiveness can hold a person in bondage even when the offender is gone. People can forgive others without telling them they are forgiven or even after they are dead. Lasting freedom comes from addressing root causes of marital conflict.

Resolving Differences through Agreement

Married couples who are experiencing conflict in their relationship are often advised to pursue agreement. Through agreement a decision on some area of the marriage is accepted by both partners. Often agreement can be reached through open discussions, consideration of relevant issues and respect between the partners. Sometimes the conflict is so deep a counselor or mediator is needed to help resolve differences and reach agreement. Even marriage counselors with natural or worldly perspectives try to help couples reach agreement. Christian marriage counselors use Biblical principles to help married couples reach agreement. They praise the power of agreement. Agreement reduces conflict and allows the couple to move forward. A husband and wife can move towards agreement in a particular area by yielding some of their self-interests.

Roots contain life. If the roots of both the husband and wife are grounded in the word of God and his love, they will produce the fruit of the Spirit. This fruit is the lasting fruit Jesus wants all to produce (John 15:16). However, if the roots are planted in selfishness, envy or strife, they will produce carnal fruit. Carnal fruit is corrupt and causes corruption in the marriage relationship.

The process of reaching agreement may appear to be the main remedy for marital problems. Still, agreement on carnal goals could destroy a marriage. More attention needs to be focused on the nature of goals in marriage.

One Spirit

The only goal for marriage that will work consistently is to pursue the kingdom of God and the will of the Father. "But seek first his kingdom and his righteousness, and all these things will be added to you" (Matthew 6:33). When the disciples asked Jesus to teach them how to pray, he said pray the Father's kingdom would come and his will would be done on earth as it is in heaven. This prayer can be applied to any marriage: May the Father's kingdom come in the marriage and his will be done in the marriage.

The expression of the Father's kingdom and his will in marriage can be called a spiritual marriage. While other marriages fail over dying love, a spiritual marriage will last throughout the years. Only a spiritual marriage has the power to sustain love beyond the beauty and strength of youth. Partners in a spiritual marriage demonstrate love in deed and not in words only. "The kingdom of God does not consist in words but in power" (1 Corinthians 4:20). The kingdom of God exists wherever the truth reigns. When the truth of God's word reigns in a marriage, it is a blessed marriage. Then God becomes fully involved in the marriage, answering prayers and solving problems.

Spiritual Agreement

Spiritual agreement in marriage involves the husband and wife coming into agreement with the will of the Father. "This is the confidence which we have before him, that, if we ask anything according to his will, he hears us. And if we know that he hears us in whatever we ask, we know that we have the requests which we have asked from him" (1 John 5:14-15). God will be involved in any marriage in which the husband and wife are in agreement and pray according to the Father's will. Their prayers will be effective.

Spiritual agreement, based on Biblical principles, is a powerful force. Jesus said, "If two of you agree on earth about anything that they may ask, it shall be done for them by my Father who is in heaven" (Matthew 18:19). Your Father hears your prayers and answers them when you pray according to his will.

When the husband yields some of his self-interests or rights to the Lord he does not lose. In fact he gains by aligning himself with the will of the Father. Likewise, when the wife yields some of her self-interests or rights to the Lord she does not lose. Rather she gains by coming into alignment with the will of the Father

Tools to Reach Spiritual Agreements

Kingdom

Repent for the kingdom is at hand (Matthew 4:17). Repent for everything done in marriage not of faith is sin. Repentance involves a change in thinking, which comes from renewing the mind to the word of God. Let the truth of God's word reign in the marriage. Accept the righteousness provided by the crucifixion and resurrection of Jesus Christ. Do what is right in the eyes of the heavenly Father.

Self-sacrifice

A godly marriage is led by the Spirit, not carnal thinking. Let the husband prefer the wife and the wife prefer the husband. "Give preference to one another in honor" (Romans 12:10b). "Be subject to one another in the fear of Christ" (Ephesians 5:21).

Unconditional Love

Love never fails (1 Corinthians 13:8). All of the requirements of a spiritual marriage are embodied in God's love. Only the greatest love is appropriate for a spiritual marriage. No man has greater love than to lay down his life for another (John 15:13). Unconditional love in marriage involves the husband laying down his life for the wife and the wife laying down her life for the husband. There is no fear in love; but perfect love casts out fear (1 John 4:18a). Unfailing love does not keep a record of wrongs suffered but covers a multitude of sins. It does not act selfishly.

Personal Story - Agreement

As a young couple, Sherry and I learned it was important for married couples to come into agreement. We did not realize agreement can be based on carnality, which is the pursuit of fleshly pleasures. Carnal thinking is hostile to God. Carnal agreements are unstable and far from the will of the Father. When our three children were ready to begin elementary school, we visited the neighborhood school but were very disappointed with the facility and teaching staff. Rather than sending our children to school there, we decided to move to another school district. We agreed to build a new home where our children could attend a better school.

We agreed on the land, the house plan, the builder and the bank loan. Although we prayed every step of the way, we did not hear directly from the Lord at first. We walked softly before the Lord, listening for his instructions. We were doing what we thought was best for our children until we heard directly from him. Then the Lord said to stay in the house in which we were living. We were confident things were going to change, because "God said it". We backed out from all agreements about the new house with other people. Then the school was rebuilt and staffed with all new teachers. It won state awards for excellence and our children received a great education there. In this case natural agreement meant nothing compared to hearing from the Lord who knew the future.

Concluding Remarks

Marital problems can result from a husband and wife having different goals and priorities. By understanding these differences, the married couple can resolve some problems. In particular, being willing to compromise and reach agreement on natural goals, a married couple can resolve some problems but not all. Many problems can never be resolved using natural means. Also, natural approaches do not provide lasting solutions to many problems. It takes the guidance of the Spirit to identify root causes of marital problems and resolve them. When the husband and wife agree to lay aside their individual and collective goals to seek the Father's will, the married couple can fulfill destiny.

Chapter 12

A LETTER TO THE HUSBAND

Through 50 years of marriage, I made many mistakes, but I learned a lot about marriage through both the good times and the bad times. People recognize Sherry and I have a wonderful marriage together. Recently, a young woman who never intended to marry completely changed her perception about marriage after seeing how we flowed together in life and ministry. Both the husband and wife can truly love each other, be anointed by the Spirit and fulfill destiny together. The purpose of this letter to the husband is to share some of the most important things I learned about marriage from revelation by the Spirit. The two areas addressed in this letter are (1) the husband's relationship with the Lord and (2) his relationship with his bride.

Bringing Forth Christ in Your Own Life

The Lord calls the husband to be the head of the marriage. "The husband is the head of the wife, as Christ also is the head of the church" (Ephesians 5:23). Marriage holds a key position in the Lord's plan, and the Lord holds the husband accountable for the marriage. Love joins a man and woman together, but marriage joins the generations together. The husband is held accountable for a great responsibility. No husband is able to meet the Lord's standard on his own; he must trust the Lord to fulfill his responsibilities as head of the marriage.

Trusting in the Lord is critical for all believers, but it is especially important for a husband because the marriage is at stake. Trusting in the Lord means following him by the Spirit. "Not by might nor by power, but by my Spirit," says the Lord of hosts (Zechariah 4:6). A husband who trusts the Lord puts things in his hands and obeys his commands. A practical way of understanding the concept of trusting the Lord is to consider the husband's rights. When the husband trusts the Lord, he puts these rights in the Lord's hands.

When a man marries he feels he has several rights (or self-interests) in the marriage. These rights may include doing the things he wants, eating and drinking what he wants, using his finances as he wants and having sex when he wants. Although other rights could be listed, these are some of the most important ones concerning marital relationships.

Consider how Jesus and his disciples dealt with their own rights. Jesus gave up all of his rights on the way to the cross when he prayed for the Father's will to be done, not his own will (Matthew 26:42). Jesus told his disciples, "If anyone wishes to come after me, he must deny himself, and take up his cross and follow me" (Matthew 16:24). The apostle Paul became a prisoner of Christ, giving up his rights (Ephesians 3:1 and Philemon 1:1 and 9). Paul instructed believers to imitate him as he imitated Christ (1 Corinthians 11:1). These are the examples a husband would follow if he really trusts the Lord.

The word of God has much to say about a husband's rights. These rights will be addressed from God's perspective using the word of God. Giving up your rights as a husband allows you to draw closer to God and do his will.

Yield to the Lord on Things to Do

Like all believers, the husband's first priority is to seek the kingdom of God and his righteousness (Matthew 6:33). Everything you do should give glory to the Lord (1 Peter 4:11). "Whatever you do in word or deed, do all in the name of the Lord Jesus, giving thanks through him to God the Father" (Colossians 3:17). Like the apostles, I give myself continually to prayer and to the ministry of the word (Acts 6:4). I live the gospel not the lie of a hypocrite.

Yield Finances to the Lord

A husband who works and earns money has the right to spend his money as he wants. Holding onto your right to spend the money as you want may keep you from tithing and giving as directed by the Spirit. I learned to give out of obedience to the Spirit rather than out of obligation. I minister the word without cost to those receiving it.

Yield Diet and Exercise to the Lord

Everything the husband puts in his body should glorify the Lord. "Your body is a temple of the Holy Spirit who is in you, whom you have from God, and that you are not your own" (1 Corinthians 6:19b). Paul disciplined his body in hardships so he would be able to stand the test of living the gospel (1 Corinthians 9:27). A husband who becomes overweight by maintaining his right to eat and drink as he pleases will not be able to carry out the Father's will over his lifetime as well as a person who keeps his mind and body fit. Also, he might not be willing to fast in order to draw closer to the Lord. The Lord instructed me to eat healthy, fast as he directs and exercise regularly. I have diligently run and hiked and eaten in moderation. Some people say I eat like a bird, but I have enough. I also fast as the Lord directs. I have even finished first in my age category in some 5-K races over the past few years. When I was a young man, a friend told me to watch out or I would gain a pound for every year of marriage. I heeded his advice and kept my weight fairly constant. I saw him years later and told him I had heeded his advice, but he had not heeded it himself. He had gained 35 pounds over 35 years of marriage.

Yield to the Lord on Sex

A husband who holds onto his right for sex whenever he wants may look for sex whenever and wherever it pleases him. This might even lead to pornography and adultery. Stewards of the Lord are required to be faithful and trustworthy (1 Corinthians 4:2). He who is faithful in little will be faithful in much (Luke 16:10). An unfaithful husband will destroy the marriage. A long time ago, I made a decision to be faithful to my wife. It was a faith-filled decision. If I had not made a decision of faith, I would have fallen for the enemy's traps.

Bringing forth Christ in Your Bride

It is important for the husband to view his wife in the proper perspective. Each woman in the body of Christ is first and foremost the bride of Christ. How does Christ view his bride? The way Christ views his bride provides guidance to the husband on how to view his own bride, because both Christ's bride and the husband's bride are one and the same person.

The bride of Christ is made up of many members, because there are many brides who have made Jesus Christ their savior. Christ is returning for a spotless and glorious bride. How can the overall bride of Christ be spotless and glorious unless every bride in the body of Christ is spotless and glorious? Every husband in the body of Christ has a great responsibility to present his own bride as spotless and glorious in order for the aggregate bride to be spotless and glorious.

Your bride's works of self-righteousness do not make her spotless and glorious. Her self-righteousness is as filthy rags to the Lord. "All our righteous deeds are like a filthy garment" (Isaiah 64:6b). The finished work of the cross makes the bride spotless and glorious. "Though your sins are as scarlet, they will be as white as snow; though they are red like crimson, they will be like wool" (Isaiah 1:18). The blood of Jesus makes her sins as white as snow. See your wife through the perfect finished work of the cross rather than her faults.

A spiritual marriage recognizes Christ within the husband and the wife. Let the Christ in you bring forth Christ in your wife and vice versa. This approach to marriage focuses on the invisible and eternal Christ operating within believers. Implementing this process focuses on Christ as the Anointed One. Hence Christ within relates to the anointing within. The Spirit lives within believers and his anointing teaches them everything they need to know, and everything he teaches is true (1 John 2:27). A spiritual marriage requires both the husband and wife to hear from the Spirit. God anointed Jesus with the Spirit and led him by the Spirit

(Acts 10:38; Matthew 4:1). If it was so important for Jesus to be anointed with the Spirit and led by the Spirit, it is certainly important for a husband and wife to be anointed with the Spirit and led by the Spirit. Those who hear and obey the Lord's commands as spoken through the Spirit will have strong faith and do exploits in life and marriage.

Personal Story - Decision-making

Our seven-year-old son, Jason, became sick and suffered much pain. We rushed him to the doctor, who said his white blood count was high, indicating an infection. He said Jason's appendix needed to be removed through surgery. We took Jason to the hospital and permitted surgery. After surgery the doctor said there was nothing wrong with Jason's appendix, but still it was removed. The infection in his body was located around his stomach, and the surgery did not address the infection. The doctor's announcement was disturbing to me; I had permitted my seven year-old son to go through unnecessary surgery. I fell on my knees in the hospital room and vowed I would not make a decision like this again without first seeking the Lord. I have an image burned in my memory of young Jason walking down a corridor wearing a hospital gown and pulling a pole with an IV bag to which he was attached. It is a vivid memory of how making decisions without first seeking the Lord can have tragic consequences.

Through the years, I have made more than my share of mistakes in marriage and raising a family. However, I have sought the Lord about decisions. Sometimes I may not hear what he says, and other times I may go ahead of him. Whenever I follow his guidance, he keeps me on the right path. He even shows me paths I did not consider. For example, he said I would be a university administrator when I had not wanted to be one, because I was satisfied with my career in research and teaching. It was his plan for me to be an administrator. Even though there was opposition against my becoming an administrator, his plan could not be stopped. I served as an administration as long as he wanted me to be one. He blessed me and my department for my obedience.

It is critical to be sensitive to the Spirit at all times. He shows you things to come and the paths on which to walk. The only way a man can justify a decision before the Lord is to know he has followed the Spirit.

Concluding Remarks

As a husband, you are called to be head of the marriage. You have to be prepared and empowered to be head of a spiritual marriage. Spiritual headship is not a right but a responsibility. As head, you are responsible for providing for your wife and family and covering them with prayers. Be vigilant to guard your wife and family from the deceptions of the world and the demonic attacks of the enemy. Establish your home as a refuge and a place of peace for you and your wife and family.

Chapter 13

A LETTER TO THE WIFE

The highest calling for women is to please the Lord. Many let marriage be a distraction or hindrance. "The woman who is unmarried, and the virgin, is concerned about the things of the Lord, that she may be holy both in body and spirit; but one who is married is concerned about the things of the world, how she may please her husband" (1 Corinthians 7:34). Do not let marriage be a distraction or a hindrance from fulfilling your purpose in life. When a married woman lives to please the Lord, he causes her husband to live peacefully with her.

Hope is in Christ and Christ alone. Without Christ people are without God and without hope (Ephesians 2:12). As a wife, your hope is in Christ, and your husband's hope is in Christ. Therefore, your greatest contribution to your marriage concerns Christ. By bringing forth Christ in your own life and in your marriage, you can strengthen the marriage. This letter examines how you can draw closer to Christ and help bring forth Christ in the life of your husband and marriage.

Bringing forth Christ in Your Own Life

Build your marriage on godly wisdom. "Wisdom is the principal thing; therefore get wisdom" (Proverbs 4:7a NKJ). See yourself as Lady Wisdom, who builds her house and furnishes her table. "Wisdom has built her house; she has hewn out her seven pillars" (Proverbs 9:1). These pillars of wisdom are identified below.

1. The beginning of wisdom is the reverent fear of the Lord (Proverbs 9:10).
2. Wisdom abounds in the presence of the Lord (Proverbs 17:24).
3. Wisdom brings life (Proverbs 3:13-18).
4. Humility receives wisdom (Proverbs 11:2).
5. Godly counsel gives wisdom (Proverbs 13:10).
6. God's discipline reinforces wisdom (Proverbs 29:15).
7. Kindness is the way of wisdom (Proverbs 31:26).

Pillars in the natural support something, such as the roof of a house. If any of the pillars is missing or broken, the whole structure would be weak. These seven pillars of wisdom can support a spiritual marriage. Fearing the Lord, receiving instruction and showing kindness are just a few of the ways these pillars can be applied in your life. All of the pillars are needed to support and strengthen your marriage. Failure to apply these pillars in your life could weaken your marriage. Make sure all of them stand firm in your life and marriage.

Identity

As a wife, your identity is in Christ, not in your husband and not in your functions of being a wife or mother. If you hide your identity in marriage or family, your husband may soon overlook you, not knowing who you really are. How will your husband value your function as a mother after your children are grown? The functions of being a wife, mother or even an income earner do not define you. You have a purpose and destiny in Christ beyond your functions in the marriage and family.

As a believer, woman, you are one of God's sons and destined to be conformed to the image of Christ. "For all who are being led by the Spirit of God, these are sons of God" (Romans 8:14). The heavenly Father has a process whereby young, immature sons mature into responsible sons with great authority. The Father loves his sons, and therefore he nurtures, instructs and trains them as sons (Ephesians 6:4). Also, he disciplines his sons (Hebrews 12:7-8). Developing a strong relationship with the Spirit will help you as a son to hear and recognize his voice. Becoming more sensitive to spiritual things is a sign of maturity. Only mature sons consistently follow the guidance of the Spirit.

Complete in Christ

No one can complete you other than Christ. In Christ you have been made complete, and he is the head over all rule and authority (Colossians 2:10). The husband does not complete the wife. As long as the wife thinks she is completed by her husband, she will be lacking something whenever her husband is not near. Thinking the husband completes the wife may lead to devastation for the woman who finds herself alone after separation, divorce or death of her husband. What happens to the wife who thinks the husband completes her when he becomes sick, disabled or mentally unstable? She may not be able to cope well with these problems. When you know you are complete in Christ, you will be able to stand against adversity.

Personal Story - Identity

When our children were young, I wrote an anniversary card to Sherry, listing some of the things I appreciated about her. I thought she would be pleased with the time and thought I put into the card. Instead, she pointed out most of the things on the list related to being a mother rather than my wife. Although I appreciate her being a good mother, I needed to love her and appreciate her for who she is rather than what she does. Marriage is not about performance.

Bringing forth Christ in Your Husband

From the beginning the wife was described as a helpmate to the husband (Genesis 2:19). Your role as a wife involves being a helpmate to your husband, his companion and his helper. This role does not imply an inferior position. The Lord intends for your husband to be the head of your marriage and for you to help him. The best way to help is to bring forth Christ, the ultimate head in your life, in the life of your husband. Only as Christ comes forth in your husband can he be the spiritual head of your marriage.

Before a husband functions as head, it is tempting for a bold and/or spiritual woman to wrongfully assume authority and act as head. She may try to justify taking control by claiming she is doing what her husband is unwilling or unfit to do or she is fulfilling the ministry to which she has been called. However, ministry is not above kingdom and marriage. Follow the Spirit in developing a spiritual marriage. This discussion provides guidance on bringing forth Christ in your husband and empowering him to take his rightful position in marriage.

Many families gratefully recognize their matriarch is like the virtuous woman described in the word of God. The attributes of a virtuous woman are worthy to be attained. A virtuous woman brings honor to her husband (Proverbs 12:4). Here is some guidance for becoming a virtuous woman. There are two important examples of the virtuous woman. First, Ruth, who followed Naomi like you would follow the Spirit, was described as a virtuous woman (Ruth 3:11). What a great impact Ruth had, because Jesus himself is listed among her descendants. Second, the virtuous woman is described in detail in Proverbs 31. She has strong character and wisdom. She has an important role in the family and makes adequate provision for family members. She covers her family with prayers and recognizes the power the Lord has given her. She is a businesswoman who buys and sells and invests her own earnings.

She has far-reaching influence. She helps her husband attain a position of great authority in their city. As you ponder the virtuous woman, the Spirit will reveal more about the attributes he is birthing and developing in you, O Virtuous Woman.

Wisdom

One of the most important goals for a wife is to bring forth Christ in her husband. Use God's wisdom to help bring your husband into God's presence as a mature person in Christ (Colossians 1:27-28).

Sherry's insights and advice are valuable to me. She is my most severe critic, correcting me when I am thinking or acting in an inappropriate way. On the other hand, she is my greatest supporter, helping me when I need help and giving encouragement when appropriate. If she was always critical or always encouraging then her advice would not mean as much as it does. Her advice is important, because I know she hears from the Spirit and she is transparent and open with her thoughts and opinions.

Prayer

The wife is often the first in a marriage to sense changing rhythms in the marriage. By being sensitive to the leading of the Spirit, you will realize when the Lord wants to move your marriage in a different direction. It is never appropriate for a wife to use either controlling or manipulative means to get the husband to behave in a particular way or move in a particular direction. The possibility of achieving a desired goal does not justify using inappropriate means to achieve it. Prayer is always needed for the married couple to follow the leading of the Spirit. As a wife, you have a great responsibility to hear from the Spirit and pray for the Father's will concerning your husband and marriage. Prayer provides a covering for your husband and ushers in God's perfect will. Prayer also empowers the husband to be the spiritual head of the house.

Personal Story - Prayer

When I am in danger, the Spirit of intercession moves on Sherry and she prays for me. One time when I was in a city several hundred miles away, I got into a taxi driven by a speed demon. I was frightened by how fast he was driving. Sherry was driving her own car with our three children in the city where we live, and the Spirit of intercession came upon her. She immediately stopped her car in a parking lot and prayed intensely for me. Back to the taxi ride, another car ran through an intersection ahead of us without stopping at a stop sign and was hit by the taxi in which I was riding. The other car was knocked into a building, because we were travelling so fast. I was sitting in the back seat with no seat belt. At impact my knees bent the full seat ahead of me into a "V" shape. I saw the driver of the other car fall out of his car, and I was very concerned about him. Miraculously, no one in the accident was injured. Sherry's intercession for me kept us all safe.

Concluding Remarks

As a wife, your marriage should be a place of safety for you, but marriages are under attack. The world is trying to redefine marriage and women's role in marriage. The enemy is trying to destroy marriages. You will have to fight for your marriage in order for it to survive. Help empower your husband to be the spiritual head, especially through prayer for him. Let your heart be established in the truth, and be led by the Spirit. Be rooted and grounded in the love of Christ. Fan the flames of fire in your marriage with unconditional love and gracious words and actions.

Chapter 14

EMPOWERMENT FOR HEADSHIP

Through the years, Sherry and I have seen more abuse and misuse in marriage over headship than any other issue. For carnal marriages, gender often appears to be the only relevant consideration for headship. There are some husbands who commit adultery, abuse their wife and fail to provide for their family but still demand to be head of the marriage. Some religious teachings use the single concept of gender to force wives to submit to their husband even in ungodly relationships. In the spiritual realm, there are many dimensions of headship. The word of God patterns the head of the marriage after Christ as head of the church (Ephesians 5:23). Christ was appointed to be head because he gave his life to purchase the church out of the world, not because he was a man. This chapter examines the requirements to be head of a spiritual marriage and the process for empowering the head.

A spiritual head is ordained by God and given the authority of God to direct the family and meet both spiritual and physical needs of the family. Only spiritual entities can have a spiritual head. A spiritual ministry can have a spiritual head, and a spiritual marriage can have a spiritual head. But a carnal marriage cannot have a spiritual head. A mixed carnal/spiritual marriage with one carnal person and one spiritual person cannot have a spiritual head. Any carnality contaminates the whole relationship: A little yeast spreads through the whole batch of dough (Galatians 5:9). If the wife is spiritual and the husband is carnally minded, the wife is still not the spiritual head according to the word of God. Even though the husband is carnally minded, the Lord still requires him to provide for his wife and family and answer for any abuse and misuse of his family.

Fit to be Head

A spiritual marriage is part of the kingdom, and it operates by kingdom principles. Those people who do not operate in the kingdom are not fit to be head of a spiritual marriage. "No one, after putting his hand to the plow and looking back, is fit for the kingdom of God" (Luke 9:62). Those people who are concerned more about worldly and carnal affairs than about the kingdom of God are not prepared to be the head of a spiritual marriage. They may operate as the head of a carnal marriage but not the head of a spiritual marriage.

The word of God has much to say about headship, including its requirements. The approach taken in this section is to consider the head of a spiritual marriage to be like a good steward. A steward is a person who is in charge of the household affairs. The steward manages or oversees the property and finances which belong to someone else. Believers are given the responsibility to steward or manage the things of the Lord. They are not their own for they have been purchased with a great price – the life and blood of Jesus (1 Corinthians 6:19 20). The Lord owns believers and the material things they possess. The Lord calls his people to the high standard of being a good steward. "As each one has received a special gift, employ it in serving one another as good stewards of the manifold grace of God" (1 Peter 4:10).

Good stewards are faithful and trustworthy. "Moreover it is required in stewards that one be found faithful" (1 Corinthians 4:2 NKJ). They discern the evil from the good and follow the things of the Lord. They choose to have no part of evil things. One passage gives several characteristics of good stewards (Titus 1:7-9). Briefly highlighting the passage, good stewards are not selfish, violent or greedy. They are hospitable, lovers of good, sensible, just and self-controlled.

This discussion focuses on who good stewards are rather than on what they do. Good stewards, being righteous, do not practice sin. God offers mercy and forgiveness to those who sometimes miss the mark of God's will. The head of a spiritual marriage will be like the good steward who is shown in the word of God.

Empowered to be Head

Believers have to be empowered with supernatural authority and power to effectively lead a spiritual marriage. When empowered, they become a transformer of God's power, releasing supernatural power into the natural realm. Believers are empowered as they mature. An immature believer is not empowered to lead a spiritual marriage. A novice is not to be placed in a position of spiritual leadership (1 Timothy 3:6). The following sections show God's provision for maturing and empowering believers.

Empowered by the Spirit

Supernatural power equips believers to do the work of the kingdom and lead a spiritual marriage. This power, which is from heaven, comes through the Spirit. The disciples were not permitted to advance the kingdom until they were given power from heaven (Luke 24:49). "You will receive power when the Holy Spirit has come upon you" (Acts 1:8). The Spirit is a storehouse of great power. As he abides in believers, they have this power in their spirit. He empowers believers to move into the supernatural realm and do exploits. This power is released by faith. Speaking the word of God and praying can cause an explosion of power.

Developing a strong relationship with the Spirit helps believers hear and recognize his voice. Becoming sensitive to his voice is a sign of maturity. "For all who are being led by the Spirit of God, these are sons of God" (Romans 8:14). Only mature believers consistently follow the guidance of the Spirit. Those who are filled with God's power are fully equipped to overcome adversities.

Empowered by the Word of God

Jesus has all authority in heaven and earth (Matthew 28:18). He delegates his authority to believers to work in his kingdom. The only kingdom authority believers have is delegated authority. This authority is revealed to them through the word of God, which is Jesus. "In the beginning was the word, and the word was with God, and the word was God (John 1:1). The word of God is powerful, and it empowers believers. "The word that God speaks is alive and full of power" (Hebrews 4:12 AMP). The amount of authority believers actually walk in depends on their understanding and applying the word.

The word of God is precious like gold. As believers act on the word, it becomes powerful to them. It will defeat every enemy and bring life, peace and prosperity to believers. All things were created by speaking the word of God in faith.

Spiritual growth involves the process of enlightenment, revelation and application. Some people are being enlightened and given revelation of the word of God but never taught how to apply it to their lives. The faith of believers becomes effective only by acting on the word. Understanding and applying the word help empower believers to be the head of a spiritual marriage.

Empowered by Spiritual Relationships

Believers are empowered with authority by being under authority to spiritual leaders. The man who recognized real authority comes from being under authority was characterized as having great faith (Matthew 8:5-13). Christ gave the five-fold ministry gifts to mature believers so they can live in harmony together. Those spiritual leaders help nurture and train believers. Spiritual leaders are responsive to the Spirit and controlled by the Spirit. They exhibit a spirit of humility as they guide believers and even restore those who have done something wrong.

A spiritual leader who takes on a nurturing role for a person over a long period of time becomes a spiritual father to him/her. Spiritual fathers have the heavenly Father's heart to bring forth sons. Joseph was a spiritual father to Pharaoh. He said, "God has made me a father to Pharaoh and lord of all his household and ruler over all the land of Egypt" (Genesis 45:8). Elijah was a spiritual father to Elisha. When Elijah was taken up in the fiery chariots, Elisha cried out "My father, my father, the chariots of

Israel and its horsemen!" (2 Kings 2:12). In the New Testament, Joseph was a spiritual father to Jesus, and Paul was a spiritual father to Timothy, Titus and others. As a spiritual father, Paul labored in prayer for those he called his children so they would mature. He desired for Christ would be manifested in their lives (Galatians 4:19).

Paul wrote spiritual fathers are rare relative to carnal leaders (1 Corinthians 4:14-15). It is easier to find a thousand carnal leaders in local congregations, than a true spiritual father. Carnal leaders may comfort and manage believers, but they cannot mature them. Carnal leaders frequently overuse the term "church family" to mask the true nature of a local congregation functioning more as a club or fraternity than a true spiritual family. Believers may survive in a local congregation being managed by carnal leaders, but spiritual fathers are needed to mature sons and bring forth Christ in them.

Believers are encouraged to mature in the Lord and be empowered to walk in authority and fulfill destiny. A spiritual father helps believers mature and can impart things into their lives that could not be obtained from anyone else. God has a spiritual father for every believer. Failure to identify and join God's ordained spiritual father will hinder a believer's spiritual growth.

Headship in marriage is strengthened by being under authority. Both the husband and wife can look to a person in spiritual authority for counsel and guidance. Any arbitrary decisions by the head can be appealed by the spouse to the person in spiritual authority over the couple. Many marital problems can be resolved with help from someone in a position of spiritual authority.

Spiritual fathers help protect families from destruction. Many families have been destroyed, because they were isolated from the body and Christ and did not recognize the importance of godly relationships. The Spirit will show a husband and wife the relationships ordained of the Lord to propel them into their destiny.

Concluding Remarks

God empowers the head of a spiritual marriage to empower others, including the spouse and the children. The best way to strengthen a marriage is to empower both the husband and the wife. They both have a stake in empowering each other.

Chapter 15
SIGNS ON PATH TO MATURITY

The path of life for a married couple leads to maturity and oneness. The Lord will show the path of life to those who desire it (Psalm 16:11). Christ-centered marriages flow with the rhythms of grace. Only those who are spiritual can know these rhythms. "May God keep us centered and devoted to him, following the life path he has cleared, watching the signposts, walking at the pace and rhythms he laid down" (1 Kings 8:58 MSG). Oneness between the husband and wife is a state of maturity reached through faith and guidance of the Spirit. Before going to the cross, Jesus prayed for believers to be one just like he was one with the Father (John 17:20-23). The work of the cross and his prayer for oneness made a way for the husband and wife to become one. The path of life is marked by signs of increasing maturity and oneness. This chapter addresses the process leading to maturity by examining different concepts of union in marriage. Each of these concepts is considered as a sign on the path to maturity.

The first signs along the path represent basic progress towards maturity, and the latter signs represent more advanced progress towards maturity. Incorporating the first concepts into a marriage will make it easier to incorporate other concepts. These concepts are the building blocks for a spiritual marriage. Readers can use these signs to assess their own progress on the path to oneness.

Preferring One Another

Both the husband and wife are highly valued in a spiritual marriage. A good way to express this value is to prefer one another. In such cases, the husband would prefer or favor his wife over himself, and likewise the wife would prefer or favor her husband over herself. Each partner would put a higher priority on the spouse's interests than his/her own. "Give preference to one another in honor" (Romans 12:10b). Selfishness cannot persist in a marriage in which both the husband and wife prefer one another.

Sherry and I have preferred one another for years. When one of us expresses a preference for something, such as movies, restaurants and travel destinations, the other one accepts this preference without any concerns. When neither of us has a preference for something, one may present several alternatives and let the other one choose. We often share a meal at restaurants, and I divide the food into two portions but allow her to choose which portion she prefers. I am satisfied with the remaining portion.

Submitting to One Another

Either spouse can submit by accepting the will of the other. It is unusual for both the husband and wife to submit to each other. However, the word of God calls for submitting one to another. Submit to one another out of reverence to Christ (Ephesians 5:21). Such a level of mutual commitment is beyond just preferring one another. Most people have a very limited view of submission, but the word of God gives clear instructions on submitting one to another. These instructions call for the husband to submit to the wife and the wife to submit to the husband. Any husband who always requires his wife to submit to him is acting contrary to the concept of submitting to one another. Considering the spouse's perspective may help the other person submit to his/her spouse.

One way to consider the concept of submitting to one another is for the wife to submit in some issues and the husband to submit in others. Over the years of our marriage, Sherry and I both think we have done more than our fair share of submitting. But our marriage is not a contest, so we have not kept track of how many times we have submitted to each other. We are both fully committed to make the marriage work through all situations.

Agreement

Agreement in a marriage is reached when both the husband and wife consent to a particular decision. In such cases the husband and wife would be in one accord. "Then make me truly happy by agreeing wholeheartedly with each other, loving one another, and working together with one mind and purpose" (Philippians 2:2 NLT). Agreement is often reached by one spouse forming an opinion and then the other one willingly accepting it. When a married couple comes into agreement, they are able to call on heaven for help. "If two of you agree on earth about anything that they may ask it shall be done for them by my Father who is in heaven" (Matthew 18:19b). "Two people will not walk together unless they have agreed to do so" (Amos 3:3 EXB). When the husband and wife are not in agreement, they are going in their own separate ways, which weakens a marriage.

For several years, Sherry and I sought to be in agreement above all else. When there was any disagreement, we would discuss the situation and try to reach agreement. We did not want to continue doing anything without agreement, because we knew the Father's blessings were poured out on couples who operated in agreement. In the last few years, we discovered agreement about anything other than the will of God would create problems. It became very important for us to first hear from the Spirit and then agree on his directions.

Unity

Unity means harmony and accord. One form of unity is similar to the unity of a winning team in sports. The players on a good team put the interests of the team ahead of their own interests. The authority of a husband and wife in unity is greater than the total authority of the two individuals. In unity there is a singleness of purpose. Make every effort to preserve the unity of the Spirit for it joins you together (Ephesians 4:3). "Put on love, which is the perfect bond of unity" (Colossians 3:14b).

Sherry and I always worked well as a team. When we were dating, she liked to help me with the cattle and horses. We helped each other complete our college degrees. Sometimes one of us worked to financially allow the other one to go to college. We were both involved in raising our three children. We continue to work together in many different areas. In ministry, working as a team is valuable. We complement each other with the different gifts the Father has given us.

Oneness

Oneness exists with the godhead – the Father, his Son and his Spirit. To help understand oneness, note Jesus is the exact expression of the Father (Hebrews 1:3). They are alike in every way. The Father's plan calls for believers to enter into this same oneness. Jesus gave his divine glory, which involves the manifestation of the Spirit, so believers might share in this divine oneness (John 17:20-23). Being one with the Spirit allows believers to share in this divine oneness. "But the one who joins himself to the Lord is one spirit with him" (1 Corinthians 6:17).

Being one with the Spirit is one of God's mysteries. Like an explosion breaks apart particles, being one with the Spirit causes the separation of good and evil. It is an implanting like a new heart implant. Those who are joined with the Spirit have an unction or anointing to know the truth (1 John 2:20). By the unction of the Spirit, they know things beyond natural understanding. Paul wanted to know Christ in a personal and intimate way (Philippians 3:10). Even when he had not fully achieved this goal, he kept pressing towards it (Philippians 3:12).

Only by being one with the Spirit can believers become one in spirit with each other. This oneness can extend to any believers, especially a husband and wife. Through the manifestation of the Spirit a married couple can live together as one in the flesh and one in the spirit. "The two become one" (1 Corinthians 6:16b MSG). Oneness in a marriage brings peace. The married couple operating in oneness will have peace in their home and in their family regardless of their natural circumstances. They will be able to impart peace into the lives of others. The world will take note of every marriage in which the husband and wife operate in oneness, because the Father's blessings will abound. Like Paul, I have not obtained the goal of being fully one with the Spirit, but I have touched it at times and continuously press towards the goal.

Concluding Remarks

By travelling along the path of life towards maturity, a husband and wife can become one in the flesh and one in the spirit. Their progress along the path causes them to become more sensitive to one another and more sensitive to the Spirit. How can anyone who is insensitive to his/her spouse think he/she is spiritual and sensitive to the unseen Spirit? With progress on the path, the husband and wife become closer together and their union becomes stronger. The fruit of the Spirit, especially love and peace, are evident along the path towards maturity. The husband and wife can progress to the place where the unction of the Spirit becomes more real to them than the natural circumstances seen around them. The blessings of the Father overtake couples who progress along this path.

Chapter 16
CONCLUSIONS: BRIDGE
TO YOUR MARRIAGE

The spiritual principles and personal experiences shared in this book are intended to help readers understand the mystery of marriage and to fashion their own marital relationship as a spiritual marriage. Understanding these principles does not substitute for a personal relationship with the Spirit. The discussions in this book expose the deception and bondage coming from man-made traditions about marriage. Armed with the truth about God's plan for marriage, a husband and wife can avoid the traps of traditions and walk in freedom.

To get the most benefit out of this book, ponder how you would answer these four questions about your marriage.

1. How do you visualize your marriage currently?
2. How do you want your marriage to be?
3. What steps can you take to help change your marriage in the desired direction?
4. How can you involve your spouse to help change your marriage in the direction in which you both agree?

Developing an action plan through the guidance of the Spirit will help improve your marriage. You may want to begin pondering the answers to these questions as you read the conclusions of the book.

Every marital relationship is unique and special, so no simple formula for a good marriage will work every time. Considering the wide ranges in ages, personalities and problems among different marriages, only the Spirit knows what needs to be done in every marriage. Always ask the Spirit for guidance before making changes in your own marriage or advising others on marriage. The Spirit is the counselor and guide.

What You Can Take from this Book

It is Time to Re-Think Marriage

The popular approaches to marriage in the world and in the church are seriously flawed and cannot be fixed. Many people view marriage in a very rigid manner. Their view of marriage never changes from the time they marry until the end of life or marriage. If everything is known and everything is static, there would be no need for the Spirit in marriage. There is no freedom in such a rigid view of marriage, because it is the Spirit who gives freedom. A rigid view does not consider the mysteries of marriage, but marriage is one of the great mysteries of God. His mysteries are revealed only by his Spirit.

The Father ordained marriage as an expression of Christ and his bride operating in the kingdom. The fruit of marriage is family, connecting the generations. Thus marriage plays a critical role in the Father's plan for his kingdom as it operates according to his principles. Kingdom authority is delegated authority. In order for a married couple to operate in kingdom authority, the husband and wife have to be joined to the body of Christ. They have authority when they are under authority themselves. Life in the body of Christ flows through the joints. Life flows between the husband and wife whom God has joined together, but life also flows through the married couple's joints with the body of Christ.

A marriage based solely on romantic love seems idealistic and wonderful. Romance sweetens any marriage, but romantic love may not stand the test of time. The marriage covenant, based on the word of God and centered on Christ, provides substance and durability to the relationship. The Lord enters the marital relationship through the marriage covenant to partner with the married couple. As a married couple faces inevitable changes, they will need to respond appropriately with the help of the Lord. The marriage covenant provides a framework to cope with any and all changes. While romantic love is limited in nature, the marriage covenant brings depth and freedom to the relationship when it is properly applied under the guidance of the Spirit. With the marriage covenant, both the husband and wife can expect freedom, abundance and fulfillment.

Most marriages are either worldly marriages based primarily on natural love or carnal marriages in the church. Few would be considered as spiritual marriages. However, spiritual marriage is God's standard for all married couples. He intended the marital relationship to become a spiritual marriage. If his standard is never proclaimed or taught, married couples could ignorantly drift in any direction.

Empowerment for Leadership

Unlike leadership in the world's system, leadership in the kingdom of God springs forth from a servant's heart. Having a servant's heart qualifies and prepares a person to lead in a variety of situations. Although only one of the marriage partners can be the head of a spiritual marriage, each one can provide leadership in different areas, such as parenting, finances, prayer, and ministry. Recognizing the strengths and weaknesses of the husband and wife and properly utilizing their respective strengths help establish a stronger marriage. When the husband allows the wife to function in her ordained areas of responsibility, she will be able to develop and fulfill destiny.

Both the husband and wife have to be empowered by the Spirit to serve one another and hence provide leadership in any area of a spiritual marriage. Until the husband and wife are empowered by the Spirit, their leadership is natural and/or carnal and wrought with inadequacies. Empowerment by the Spirit yields great spiritual authority. Both the husband and wife should seek to empower each other through prayers and speaking the word of God.

Rhythms of Grace

There are static approaches to marriage in which everything is thought to be set in place and clearly known from the beginning. Typically, worldly and carnal marriages arc static in nature. With a static approach to marriage, a husband and wife would think they know everything about marriage from the time they wed until the end. Static approaches to marriage do not make allowances for change, learning to occur and guidance by the Spirit. Also, there would be no need for prayer or counsel about marriage, because the husband and wife think they understand everything about marriage. Even though this may be an oversimplification, static approaches to marriage are widespread. A more insightful approach to marriage would allow for changes and growth, denoting a dynamic process. In such cases, prayer, learning, counsel by godly believers and guidance by the Spirit are very important.

The dynamic approach to marriage examined in this book involves the rhythms of grace. There are both natural and spiritual rhythms. While the natural rhythms are easier to understand and address, the spiritual rhythms are more important in the areas of eternal purposes and fulfilling destiny. Grace rhythms follow the Spirit, so these spiritual rhythms can be understood only by guidance from the Spirit.

The seasons of marriage and the rhythms of grace are weaved throughout the book to help explain the dynamic nature of a spiritual marriage. Following these rhythms brings harmony with the Spirit and harmony between the husband and wife.

What You Can Apply from This Book

A husband and wife having different goals where marriage is concerned can be a major reason for marital conflicts. These conflicts can be resolved on a short-term basis by reaching agreement in important areas. Regardless of how much the husband and wife desire agreement and how well they communicate about it, carnal goals will continue to create marital problems over time. The only approach to marriage providing a lasting solution to conflicts involves seeking the goals and purpose of the Father and his will in marriage.

In a spiritual marriage, Christ operates freely through both the husband and wife. The Lord is looking to the husband, as head of the marriage, to bring forth Christ in himself and in his bride. No husband can fulfill this purpose on his own. He would have to trust the Lord and develop a strong relationship with the Spirit. The rewards of a marriage fashioned in heaven are great, reaching throughout the ages.

The following 25 traits of a spiritual marriage briefly highlight some important conclusions from this book. The chapters addressing these traits are shown in parentheses. A spiritual marriage:

1. Seeks first the kingdom (1)
2. Births life and continually changes (1)
3. Is energized and liberated by the Spirit (1)
4. Moves by the Spirit (2)
5. Grows in grace (2)
6. Exalts the Lord (2)
7. Discovers purpose and fulfills destiny (3)
8. Honors the marriage covenant (4)
9. Sustains love (5)
10. Endures to the end and is saved (5)
11. Cherishes intimacy even beyond sex (6)
12. Always believes (7)
13. Fights spiritually from a position of victory (7)
14. Quickly forgives (8)
15. Goes beyond traditional approaches to marriage (9)
16. Readily agrees with the Father's will (10)
17. May fall short repeatedly but never fails (11)
18. Abundantly produces lasting spiritual fruit (11)
19. Finds identity in Christ (12)
20. Gives thanks (12)
21. Prays earnestly and releases much power (13)

22. Is empowered to lead (14)
23. Serves others (14)
24. Builds spiritual relationships in the household of faith (14)
25. Presses toward maturity and oneness (15)

The details leading to these conclusions were examined in earlier chapters of the book. What are the most important conclusions relative to your own marriage?

What Results You Can Expect

Reap the Rewards of a Spiritual Marriage

Marriage is filled with rich treasures and the joy of heaven when Christ rules. These treasures of marriage cannot be comprehended by either the natural mind or the carnal mind, because they are included in the great mystery of marriage. No romance novel, television show or movie can adequately capture the mysteries of the Spirit. If these treasures could easily be discovered by worldly and carnal people, then God's plan for marriage would not be considered a great mystery. These treasures are revealed by the Spirit to any husband and wife who diligently seek the kingdom of God and his righteousness. It takes a personal relationship with the Spirit to understand the great mystery of marriage.

Fulfill Destiny

Both the husband and wife are destined to be conformed to the image of Christ and to be joined together as one in body and one in spirit. Their separate destinies become interwoven to create one new destiny, greater than anything either spouse could think or imagine alone. Through the guidance and strengthening of the Spirit, the two become one spirit with one destiny.

Every creature produces after its own kind. Those who are carnally minded produce others who are carnally minded; and those who are spiritually minded produce others who are spiritually minded. Those who are spiritual judge all things and discern the difference between carnal and spiritual things. Spiritual believers do not have to be married to produce others who are spiritual, but those who are spiritual and live in a spiritual marriage produce others who are spiritual.

Who is in a better position to assess a person's skills in relationship building than his/her own spouse? If a person cannot build a spiritual relationship at home, how can he/she build a spiritual relationship elsewhere? Every spiritual marriage is important in the kingdom of God, because it is the birthplace of spiritual relationships in the body of Christ. It is a place where a man and woman are trained to build, nurture and sustain spiritual relationships. A husband and wife can develop the necessary skills to work with spiritual relationships in the kingdom by applying their skills and having these skills tested in their own spiritual marriage.

Building solid spiritual relationships is rooted in the Father's heart. He wants a spiritual relationship with every believer, and in turn, he wants them to have spiritual relationships with each other. Spiritual people see the Father's purpose in their own lives and in the lives of others.

Those who are spiritual
Call unto the deep things of others,
Release their purpose and
Help them fulfill destiny.

www.FredAndSherryWhite.com

www.ingramcontent.com/pod-product-compliance
Lightning Source LLC
Chambersburg PA
CBHW031319040426
42443CB00005B/144